NEUROSCIENCE
APPLIED TO
SOCCER

PRACTICAL PROPOSAL

100 DRILLS FOR TRAINING

Manuel Jesús Crespo García

Title: NEUROSCIENCE APPLIED TO SOCCER. PRACTICAL PROPOSAL. 100 DRILLS FOR TRAINING

Author: MANUEL JESÚS CRESPO GARCÍA
Text correction: MANUELA CASTILLO SOLER

Publisher: WANCEULEN EDITORIAL
Collection: WANCEULEN EDITORIAL DEPORTIVA

ISBN (Paper): 978-84-18486-41-8
ISBN (Ebook): 978-84-18486-42-5

Legal deposit: SE 1088-2020

Printed in Spain. 2020

WANCEULEN S.L.
C/ Cristo del Desamparo y Abandono, 56 - 41006 Sevilla
Web: www.wanceuleneditorial.com y www.wanceulen.com
Email: info@wanceuleneditorial.com

PROLOGUE

Olympic Games, world games, Pan American games, South American games, national championships, soccer at school, on the street, in clubs, no matter the context, nor where or when, since in any of them, teachers and soccer coaches understand our human nature. What is even more difficult, "knowing how to do" classes and training sessions is decisive so that the experience is positive in both the well-being and the performance of the player, understanding the performance as the possibility of what we do, meets the objectives we want (recreational, training or performance goals).

Educating us from the neurosciences applied to the sport, is a challenge that more and more coaches and teachers are doing every day. The speed with which research comes out daily on new studies about the brain, the body and the motor action, means that if we do not study them, we will become decontextualized. Manuel Crespo, in this book, not only contributes to the development of knowledge of this subject, but achieves something that few coaches and teachers are doing in recent years: transferring science to practice.

In this book the author proposes an important challenge: to provide quality to education, to put first the learning and knowledge of our own organism, to learn about the role of attention, the functioning of our systems, on how our own brain structure... is directly involved in the quality of the "teaching-learning" process, and how It provides us with tools , exercises and explanations that will allow us to better exercise our practice as teachers. This is directly related to our ethics and quality as teachers and coaches, as it allows us to know what is happening with what we propose to our students. It gives us the foundation to put the student at the center of the process. And, at the same time that we will know ourselves more, we will better identify our internal processes, our brain functioning, anatomy, functions, and thus get to know each other more and help us generate ideal learning conditions, that improve educational contexts, that promote the focus of learning in a context based on science and experience.

I believe that this proposal can bring about changes in professionals and apprentices, and will make possible new publications and new studies. More importantly, it will lead to an improvement in the quality of education, through sport, movement and mainly through soccer.

José Pedro Riveros Santis
Elite Athletes Coach
Master in Education
Mentor High Performance Coach in Sport

INDEX OF CONTENTS

INTRODUCTION

Neuroscientist and researcher Fabricio Ballarini, talks about "neuroscience research tells us that we remember and know about the novel events, those that disrupt the routine" ... "you have to educate the brain."

"Sports neuroscience is practical, it has to do with spotlights, retention times, how to manage stress... it's an experimental thing"

Neuroscience is a scientific area that studies the nervous system throughout its scope. Neuroeducation is the application of neuroscience to learning, and studies how the nervous system works when we learn. Educational neuroscience studies the process through which our brain learns based on genetics, environment and experience, along with cognitive processes and emotions, and also studies what feelings influence learning.

There is a very strong educational tendency entrenched in these concepts, and every day is reflected in the teaching of sport, although misunderstood can lead to errors, and to not achieve the intended results. The decision-making process is:

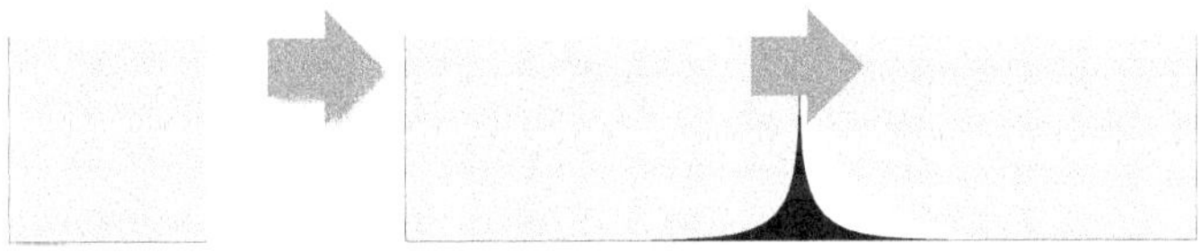

But in sports like soccer, where many decisions are made in every action, the reality is changing and the soccerer is under competitive stress in his development and learning (testosterone and cortisol appear) and the mechanism of our brain has to respond to different situations without the possibility of thinking what is the best solution. Experience and control of emotions will make the mechanism:

We will understand by stimulus the perception of what is happening, using the senses to decide more precisely, but without the possibility of reflecting to give an answer.

In Efficientsoccer.com, Professor Francisco Seirul-lo says about decision-making in soccer:

Decision-making theorists go through three phases: perception, execution and decision-making. When they have to make complex decisions, they do that. First perceive the environment, observe it, analyze it; make the decision and execute it. But in soccer there is only one situation: an idea that must be transformed into execution. There's only one phase. It's not three.

In soccer there is only one: execute an idea. Do I want to outdo you? Execution of the idea. I don't think about how I'm going to beat you. I've talked to Messi about this, many times. And he, when he wants to take his rival (...) (his idea) is to leave him nailed and take the ball elsewhere (...) He doesn't think how he'll do it. Just execute an idea. He doesn't think, he doesn't plan. Runs.

You have to know how to focus on what's important, to be selective.

Developing neuroplasticity requires different types of memory:

- **Declarative memory:** ability to remember events, numbers, sensory stimuli and storytelling.
- **Procedure memory:** ability to execute complex motor actions learned previously.

Coaches need to try to develop effective intelligence.

When we try to explain the ins and outs of the game, we tend to crumble it so we can understand it, and thus improve our argument about why we do one or the other in our methodological routine.

In any area of life, when a situation fails, it is repeated over and over until it goes well, improving execution. But a soccer match has a peculiarity that makes it different from any other activity or sport: there are no two different situations that are repeated in time. A soccer player is constantly making decisions in front of different scenarios. Until the execution of a penalty, it is an action that changes according to: the goalkeeper in front of him, the pitcher, the state of the pitch, the minute of the match, the result of the match, if it is the first one that throws or has already thrown others during the same... No two penalties are the same. I can learn from the mistakes I make so that I don't make them again, and when I encounter the same situation, my knowledge and ability to rule out non-relevant stimuli, and my ability to identify relevant stimuli, will help me to achieve the result I intend.

So how do we train the players? If whatever I do I'm never going to be able to simulate what's going to happen in the game...

Any action requires an interpretation of what is happening, but it cannot be reflective, because there is no time to value. If the player stops to reflect, he will lose advantage. Coaches have to give them tools to make their execution effective and for the player to be efficient. Goals are equally worth with the toe, as with the inner edge of the foot.

To say that soccer is played with your feet, it's like thinking that chess is played with your hands. When a player misses a pass in a match, it may be because he has mis-executed; but it may also be because he became nervous about the pressure of the opponent and rushed, because he did not wear the right footwear for the surface on which the match was unfolding, because the partner made it late to uncheck, because he chose a teammate who was marked or offside, because the opponent anticipated his action...

How do we correct this?

Severing the two teams in an action simulation explaining to the player in question how or where he should have executed the pass, I consider him a waste of time and energy that will not produce any improvement in the player or the team. You have to give it a quick and concise feedback and continue with the following. Likewise, after this, putting one player in front of another (vis a vis) and making a high number of pass replays to correct what happened to look for an improvement of the collective game is still of little use, because the routine situations are forgotten.

You learn to pass the ball, passing it over and over again in different situations, getting it right and making mistakes.

So, we have to prepare the player to be able to solve all the actions of the game, because maybe what was wrong was not the execution of the pass, but other factors related to the circumstances of the action. What we have to do is prepare players to be able to solve game situations.

The tendency to correct a mistake is to work it in isolation for performance improvement, but the experience and understanding of the game as an indissoluble unique reality, suggests that this path does not produce an improvement in the collective game, produces an improvement of an isolated action, which will never be repeated again during the player's sporting life.

To achieve the perfection of the game models, the coaches tend to crumble the game with principles, subprinciples, more subprinciples... that allow us to explain how our team plays, and this often causes our workouts to be lost in improving isolated technical factors, that we think are the ones that make players err. And it may be, to give an example, that our game model is asking our players for technical qualities that they don't have, and that it doesn't allow them to show their talent, or to make the right decisions.

Many peers do not like to teach other coaches in courses; i, on the other hand, enjoy and am very enriched to engage with colleagues who have opinions other than mine.

Aren't we, the coaches, too focused on methodology, loads, periods... and we don't realize that the protagonist is not the training, but the player? Don't we have to get the "good soccerer" out instead of chasing the player to do the best training?

In stages of training we like to teach young soccerers what hit is like for the execution of the short pass, for example. The good soccerer that we all want to have in our team, is the one who knows when to make a pass instead of driving, the one who executes the pass well, the one who interprets the action of a teammate, who anticipates the game of the opposite... in short, the one who makes the decisions well on the pitch.

We coaches are "slaves" to our methodology, training periods and competition schedules. The essence of soccer brings with it the game, a game that has to be for the player. Professor Julio Garganta talks about talent as something that is not discovered, it is achieved. Talent must be empowered and valued. *"Talent doesn't find it like a metal detector, which beeps when you have it in front of you"* (Julio Garganta).

The coaches *"... we're not exercise makers. Training is making the game feel. Each task must involve knowledge of the game..."* (Óscar Cano, 2010).

When we train our teams we have to design our training sessions. Nowadays a multitude of tasks are done trying to "disturb" the decision and condition the player in their decision-making: changing the color at the last moment that tells him where to throw, say a number and has to move to a place, touch the whistle and finish the play... I wonder why in a "game" like soccer, involving so many factors that we want the player to dominate and know how to interpret at all times, the stimuli that we use for the player to execute in training, have nothing to do with the game.

During the game different cognitive processes are coordinated simultaneously with peripheral vision.

Peripheral vision is important, but knowing how to focus on what is relevant is key to the right decision-making. There are a large number of jobs applied from the area of physical preparation, but they are far removed from the "game" itself.

In all facets of soccer we try to copy things from other sports that may be more advanced or have a higher degree of study and demonstrate transfer. Soccer is different. Situations are never repeated in the game, no two passes are the same in a match, no two shots are the same in a match, no two attacks are the same in a match... So, wouldn't it be better to prepare our team to react better to the situations that occur in the game and to stimuli that have to do with this, and not with colors, numbers, pats, whistle beep...?

By this I do not mean that there are no activation games, that these kinds of tasks are not done that can serve us to entertain the players or as team dynamics, I just express that, if we want to train soccer and make more of the trainings, those that do not have many hours to be able to train our teams we have to try to make our tasks have the greatest transfer to the game possible.

It will always be better to work so that our team in a drill, goes on to attack when the opposing team loses the ball, that it makes a pass when there is a move to uncheck the teammate, that puts pressure when the opposing team reaches an area... and we will get greater transfer to our game, depending on the team where we are, the age or ability of the players we train and the game model that we want to develop with our team.

You could argue that these stimuli attempt to "annoy" the player to train the ability to focus on what he is doing. But they are stimuli that you will never encounter during the game.

What if we put the soccer player to pass the ball to players who try to uncheck? Some will make it and some won't. The player will have to identify what is the stimulus (well unchecked player) to which he has to react and pass the ball with advantage to receive, discarding all other stimuli (unchecks that were not achieved). And if the player is also being pressured by an opposing player, or other players are crossing in between, or we place a goalkeeper for the player who receives the pass to score, or we demand that if the pass fails he has to press to pass again... you can increase the cognitive load of what you're training using elements of the game. Stimuli among which the player will have to select one, and to which he will have to react and give an answer.

In this way we will be able to contextualize the actions, to the point that we consider it necessary and taking into account the level of the players to which we are going to expose the tasks. Controlling and adapting cognitive loads.

Cognitive load theory explains that learning a task requires the recruitment of neural resources, such as attention and working memory. If the task consumes an excessive level of these resources the information will not be processed in its entirety, resulting in a decrease in learning., (Pass, Van Gog y Sweller, 2010; Shuggi, Oh, Shewokis y Gentili, 2017).

We have to try as coaches, that training is a means of facilitating learning.

Our objective as coaches is to help our players in their learning process either in training, starting or in high performance, competing. In soccer, no matter how much we try to make the competition as healthy and educational as possible in its initiation, in a match you compete with an opponent to beat him, because it is inherent in the game itself. Stimuli and responses have to be aimed at learning the player and have to be closely related to what can happen in a match for learning to be meaningful, either a situation in which the answer is always the same (for example, passing) and that decision is how to pass (long or short), or a situation in which there are many answers (counterattack) and many possible decisions within that response (there can be infinite in the execution).

To do this, the complexity of the drill will be closely related to the learning capacity and the development of the player's or team's abilities.

The most analytical tasks in learning are used for technical gesture improvements. To increase their transfer to the game, they must also demand a decision-making. Teaching the dissocied technical gestures of all the game variables, prepare the player to have dexterity in a given hit, but not to apply that action to the game variables. The reality is that players are constantly making decisions during a match, adapting to the changing reality of the game.

Two soccer players, one in front of each other, passing the ball 15 meters away; that's a task that will only give the player an improvement of the pass at that precise distance and learning will lack any cognitive improvement. If in that same task the teammate varies the distance, varying the speed at which he moves, returning the ball to different heights, moving between cones, changing spaces... or any other variable, the decision about the ball pass will be different, and the learning process will carry a higher cognitive load, that directly impacts the player's improvement in terms of the answers in the game.

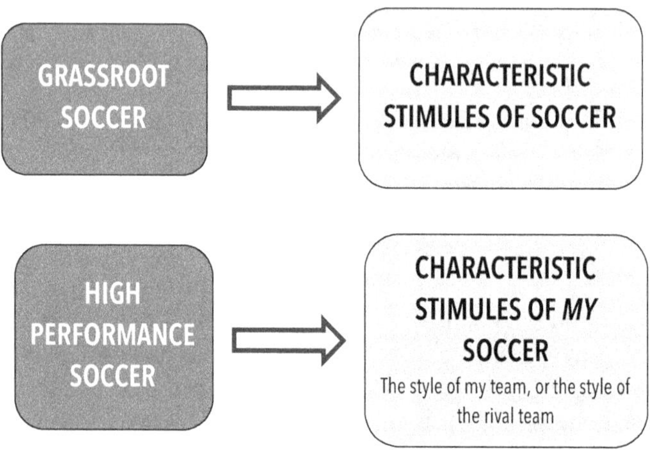

Ideally, in training our game model, the task will be conditioned by the most specific factors that will appear in the match, so that there is an experience in learning, and the response is better and faster.

There are many rules to cause the tasks and trainings to have the required result and that in the training happens what we want to happen, and thus link the objectives with the contents.

To get what we're looking for in training, I propose three types of variables factors:

- Human factors.
- Space-time factors.
- Rules factors

Using these factors, we'll get our tasks to reproduce the situations we want and transfer to the game. Let us remember that these factors cannot be artificial, they must come from the game itself.

When we want to introduce **human variable factors**, we will use the human resources at our disposal to contextualize the training. For example, if I face a team with tough defenders, I will put in all the actions in which I want my team to work the ball phase, defenses with those characteristics.

A second option is to use **space and time variable factors**. For example, if we face a team with tough defenders, we could reduce the spaces in which tasks will be performed, so that more situations occur in which players learn to make the best decision in front of those defenders.

A third option is to use rules variable factors, causing what we want to happen, introducing special rules into the tasks. In this case, we could introduce the rule that the first foul made, is not marked, causing the team that has the ball to play faster to avoid the opponent's hard contacts.

Of the three types of variable factors, the one that brings the soccerer closer to the reality of the match, is the human condition, since it makes it closer to the competition and more real, because of the unpredictable of the human factor.

When talking about space and time, and with the advent of the so-called "position style" that has been imposed in recent times, there is a question about the importance of dominating one aspect or another (space or time) to be superior in a match, and to impose our game on the contrary.

The two factors seem important to me to be able to impose ourselves on the rivals. The mastery of time is important because it will condition the effectiveness of the occupation of spaces. And the mastery of spaces is important because it will help a better interpretation of the times.

Speed is considered in its different versions: reaction, execution, decision, adaptation, gesture, movement... as a determining factor at a competitive level.

Speed is directly related to these two factors: space and time. In soccer you don't win just by doing things quickly, you win by doing things "right" or better than the other team, at the speed needed to outper't get over your opponent. You can be less quick than an opponent, but get to the ball first, you can be faster than the opponent and not be able to snatch the ball... so speed is going to be decisive in specific situations that are required, but the purpose of soccer is not to be faster, but to score more goals than the opposing team. You face an opponent and the goal is to beat him on the scoreboard, to score more goals in a given time.

Speed in all its forms, be it reaction speed, execution speed, gestural speed, decision speed... it is the quality that makes players "different", and is a very genotype-conditioned factor. This is not to say that speed cannot improve with training, but that the level of improvement is lower than in other respects, and that it may have a greater or lesser development in some individuals than in others, depending on physical factors of genetic origin.

However, the one who arrives before the ball, will be able to start the play; the one who arrives earlier, prevents the ball from entering the goal; that is, those who arrive earlier, are closer to victory. Therefore, the good interpretation of the specific speed of the game will make a team win or lose a match, and it will help us to be superior to the opposing team. The equation that makes us decisive is: rival-time-space. According to A.Wanceulen Ferrer, A.Wanceulen Moreno, J.F.Wanceulen Moreno in 2008: In high-performance soccer speed is decisive, it makes all differences. And I would add: the specific speed of the game against an opponent.

So what do we have to master in soccer? space or time? The answer is that you have to dominate the opponent, taking advantage of the spaces and time, because the meter will not be the speed itself, but the speed with respect to the opponent. Players or strategies that best take advantage of the spaces, and manage the time better in the matches, will be the most competitive. Hence, the importance of correctly identifying what are the indicators in the development of the game, because they will help us to identify faster what is happening and will activate individual and collective functions coordinated in space and time conditioned by the rival.

By applying the concept of neuroscience to soccer, we do not seek to make soccerers faster (although they will be faster in the decisions they make and in the time it takes to make them). What we are looking for is that the decision-making mechanism they develop, makes them able to decide well in the necessary time regarding the situation they have to resolve, and about the rival they face, based on their perception, knowledge and experience.

It consists of applying theories of learning to the practice of training.

It is not admissible that after so much research by specialists in physical preparation and teaching, training tasks continue to use stimuli that have nothing to do with the game, and generate contexts that are far from the competitive reality that the player will face during matches.

Dr. Robin Jackson, a professor at Brunel University, scanned a group of professional soccerers and put them on a test called a "body occlusion test." He conducted that test to find out how players anticipate the actions of their opponents. The "mirror neurons" system was the source of the ability to anticipate. Adaptive ability can be trained, just like any other skill.

The proposal, in accordance with the above, is a practical application of neuroscience (something scientific) to training (something practical) for the improvement of our players, adapted to each age or formative stage, helping us with the scientific basis provided by studies of brain behavior during sports learning.

Thus, applying the benefits of neuroscience, the indicators and stimuli that we use in the training tasks, will be the own of soccer, so that there is a greater transfer. There is a very strong educational trend entrenched in these concepts and every day is reflected in the teaching of sports. But, this trend, if not interpreted well, can lead to errors and not achieve the intended results. The goal is that the training of our brain is related to soccer, and that the skills or advances that are achieved have a direct impact on during the game.

The coach will have to condition the training drills, using the variable factors of space and time, to get the required result.

It should be noted that in the development of learning there are different stages (due to the evolution of the players). Therefore, the coaches will have to take as a reference the cognitive capacity of the players, in order to be able to choose correctly, and adapt the tasks to each formative stage.

Even if the tasks have a technical or tactical objective, that will not be the important thing. The purpose of the tasks is that there is a training of our brain so that the decision in the face of stimuli or adversities gives us an effective motor response, regulated by emotions, and that players know how to focus the important thing with an interpretation that leads them to decide without reflecting, on the fly, intuitively, and that all of this will lead to learning.

Most of the tasks that come next will be for pass improvement, driving, shooting and control, thinking about the initiation of learning as an example of the proposal. At the end of them I will develop some with defensive objectives, and other more complex objectives, to exemplify that can be carried out in learning any content, the game model, the strategy of a match, or for the development of the game in general.

SIMBOLOGY

TEAM A PLAYERS	
TEAM B PLAYERS	
TEAM C PLAYERS	
PLAYER DISPLACEMENT	
DIRECTED FIRST TOUCH	
BALL DISPLACEMENT	
BALL DRIVING	
BALL DISPLACEMENT MID-HIGH	
SHOT	
BALL	

NEUROSCIENCE
APPLIED TO SOCCER

100
DRILLS FOR TRAINING

Drill N° 1	Main Objective	Pass improvement
	Number of players	2

Explanation

Players pass the ball to the right or left of the cone in front of them, depending on where the partner is moving.

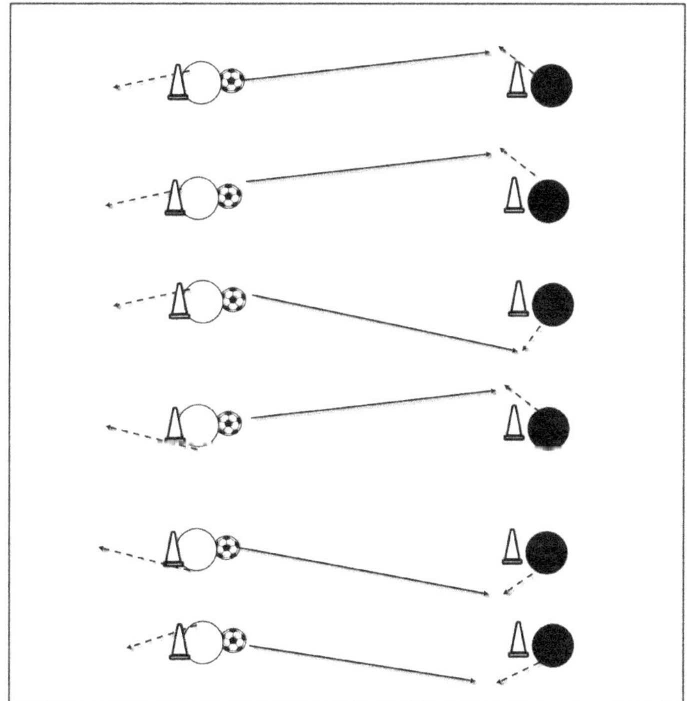

Drill N° 2	Main Objective	Pass improvement
	Number of players	2

Explanation

Players pass the ball in pairs, in short or long pass, starting from the cone and depending on where the partner is moving.

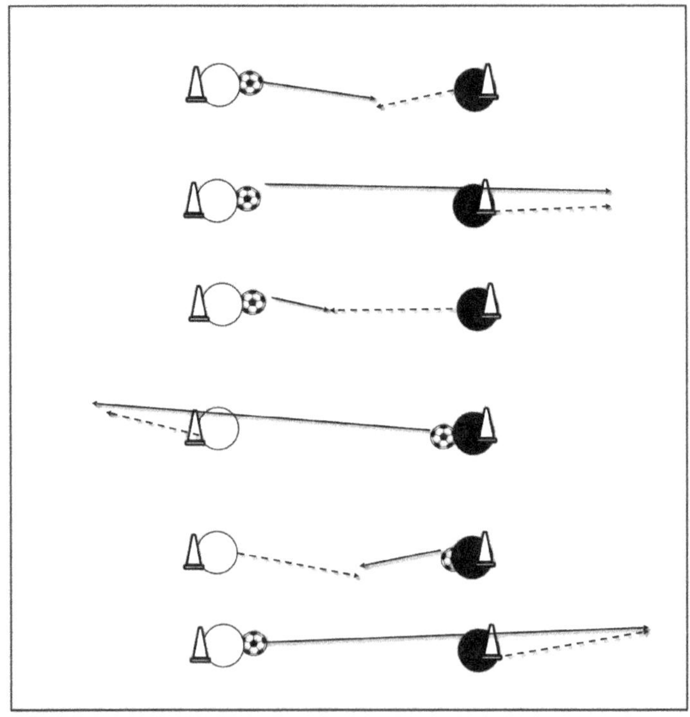

Drill N° 3	Main Objective	Pass improvement
	Number of players	7

Explanation

Players as shown in the picture. The sequence of pass: 1-2-1-3-4-5-4-6-7. Always departing behind the cone, to which they advance, they leave the cone on the right or left (randomly), well profiled to receive and pass.

Rotation will be 1-2-3-4-5-6-7.

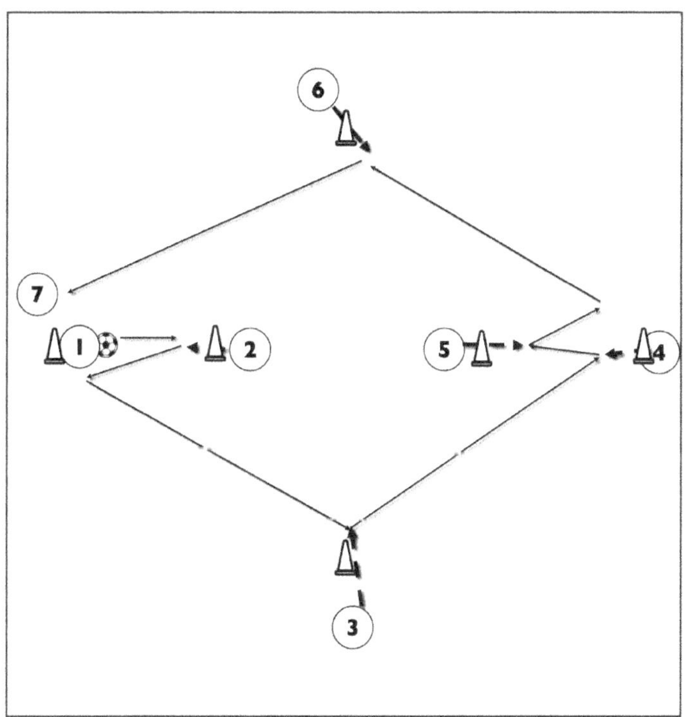

Drill N° 4	Main Objective	Pass improvement
	Number of players	5 (1x4)

Explanation

Players as shown in the picture. 1 in the square. A player make support or deep uncheck, receives from 1, returns the ball to 1 and returns to his cone. Repeat con the others players.

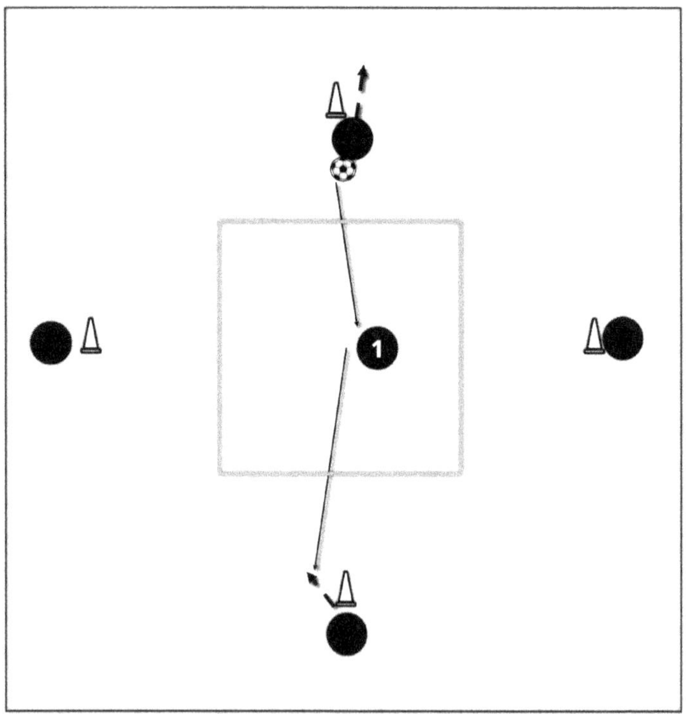

Drill N° 5	Main Objective	Pass improvement
	Number of players	11

Explanation

Players as shown in the picture. 1 in the square. A player unmarked pass the ball to 1, and 1 turns around and passes to other player unmarked. Unmarked players will vary.

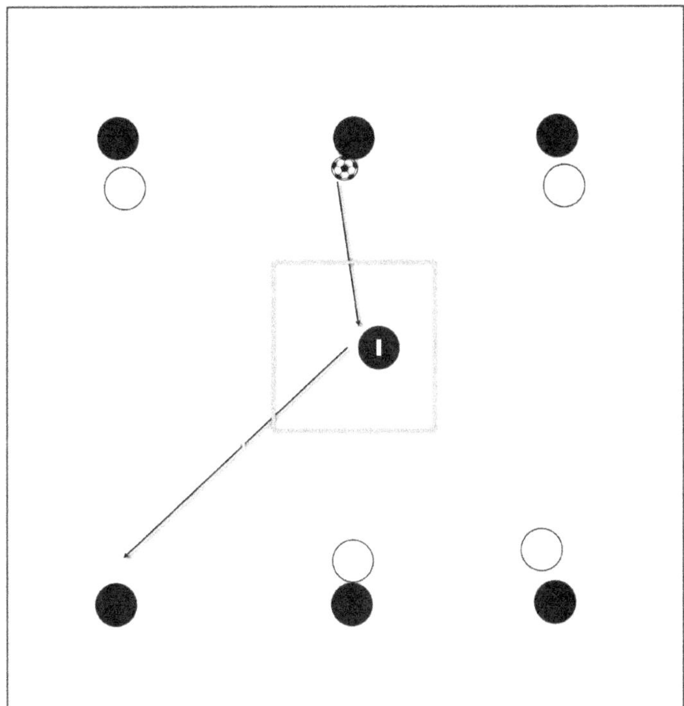

Drill N° 6	Main Objective	Pass improvement
	Number of players	15

Explanation

Players as shown in the picture. 1 in the square. A player unmarked pass ball to 1, and 1 turns around and passes to other player unmarked. Unmarked players will vary.

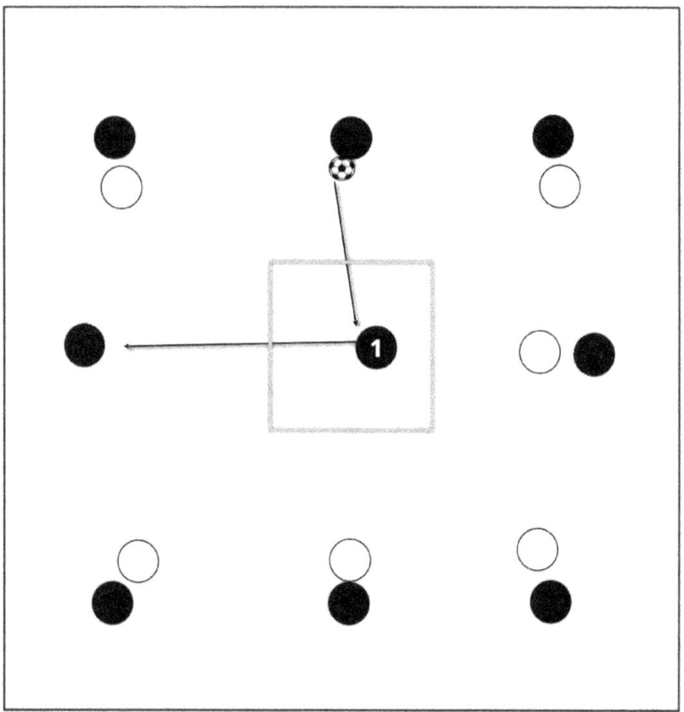

Drill N° 7	Main Objective	Pass improvement
	Number of players	15

Explanation

Players as shown in the picture. 1 in the square. A player make an support uncheck to receive, and return ball to 1. Repeat with another. Unmarked players will vary.

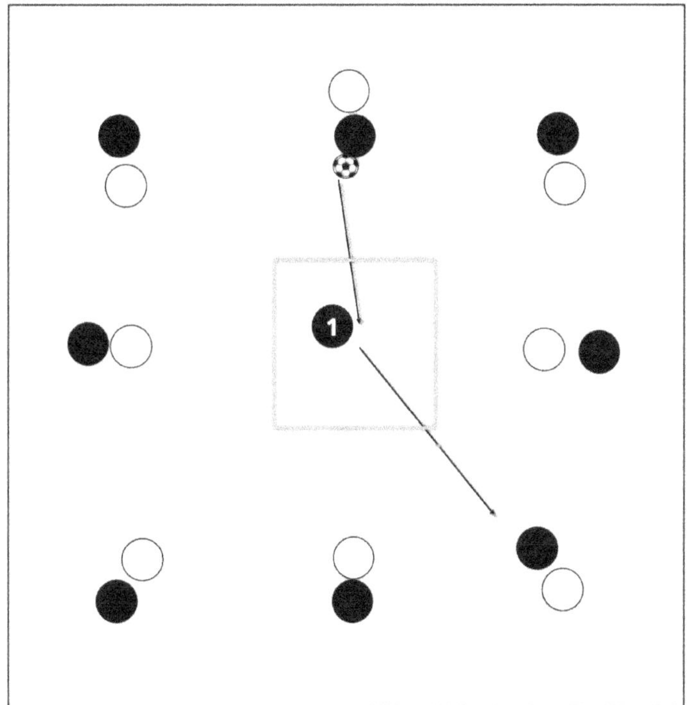

Drill N° 8	Main Objective	Pass improvement
	Number of players	17

Explanation

Players as shown in the picture. 1 in the square. 2 goes to 1, 3 unchecks and then 4 goes to press 1. When 3 receives, he returns the ball to 1, and 4 returns to his place. Repeat with the rest of the players.

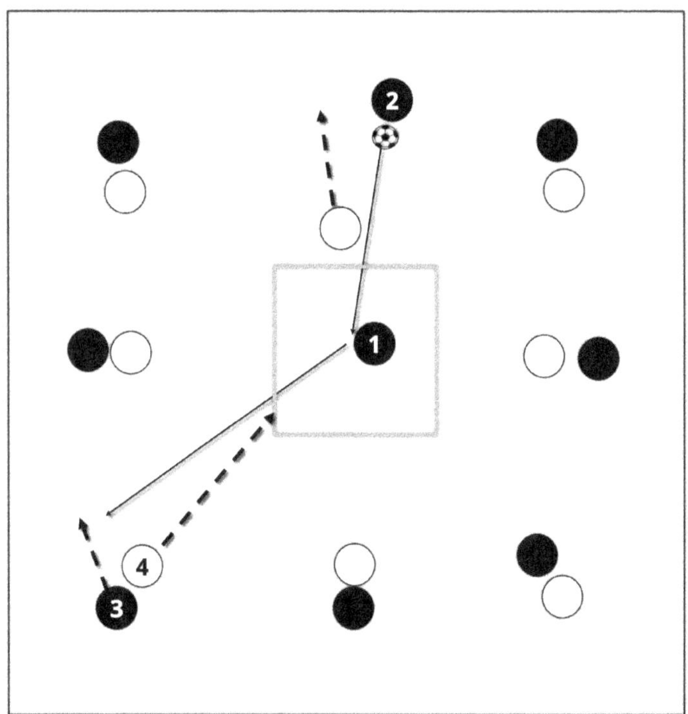

Drill N° 9	Main Objective	Pass improvement
	Number of players	21

Explanation

Players as shown in the picture. 1 in the square. Rest of players moving around the field, and trying to uncheck. 1 passes to an free player. If the pass is successful, change roles.

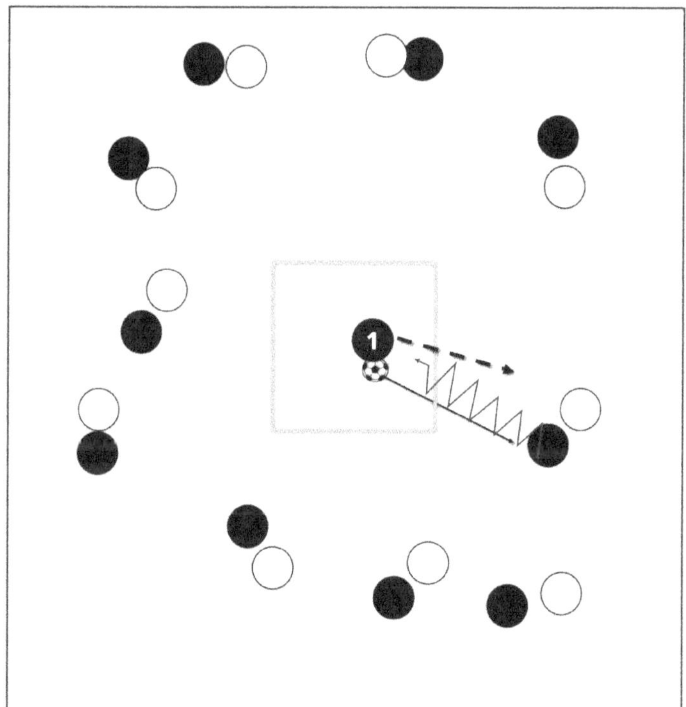

Drill N° 10	Main Objective	Pass improvement
	Number of players	21

Explanation

Players as shown in the picture. 1 in the square. The rest of players moving with man-to-man marks. When a player go to into the square and press to 1, 1 pass to unchecked player. Change roles.

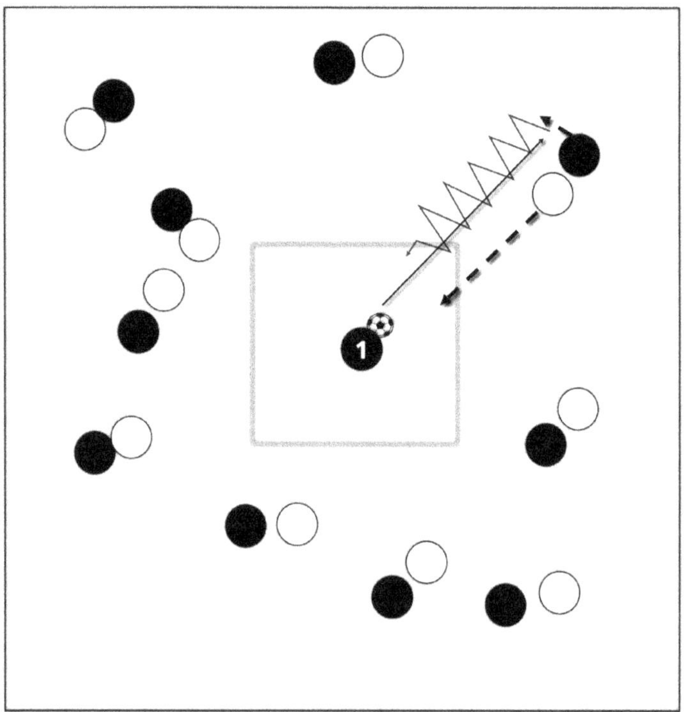

Drill N° 11	Main Objective	Pass improvement
	Number of players	13

Explanation

Players as shown in the picture. 1 in the square. When 1 receives, a player unchecks (support or deep), receives and returns ball to 1, and returns to initial position. Repeat with the other players.

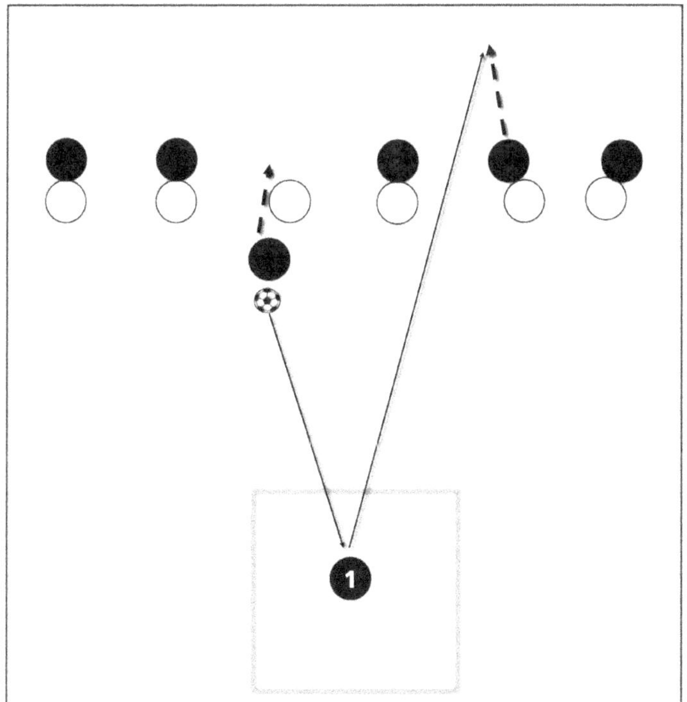

Drill N° 12	Main Objective	Pass improvement
	Number of players	17

Explanation

Players as shown in the picture. 1 in the square. When 1 receives, a player makes an unmarking (support or deep), receives and returns ball to 1, and returns to initial position.

When 1 receives, a player of the vertices will press so that it cannot pass, alternating in each action the one who does it.

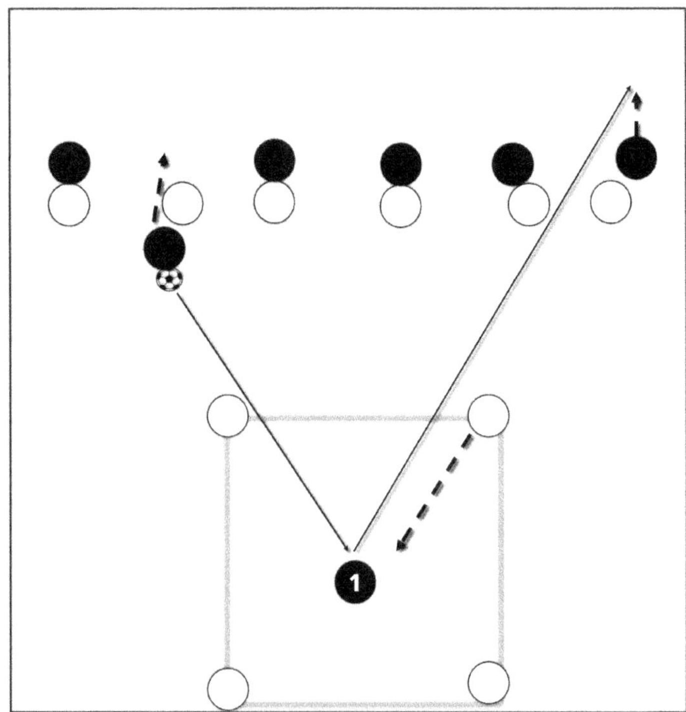

Drill N° 13	Main Objective	Pass improvement
	Number of players	4

Explanation

Players as shown in the picture. Players pass the ball and they will occupy the angle that is free. Players must be well profiled always and in a position to receive.

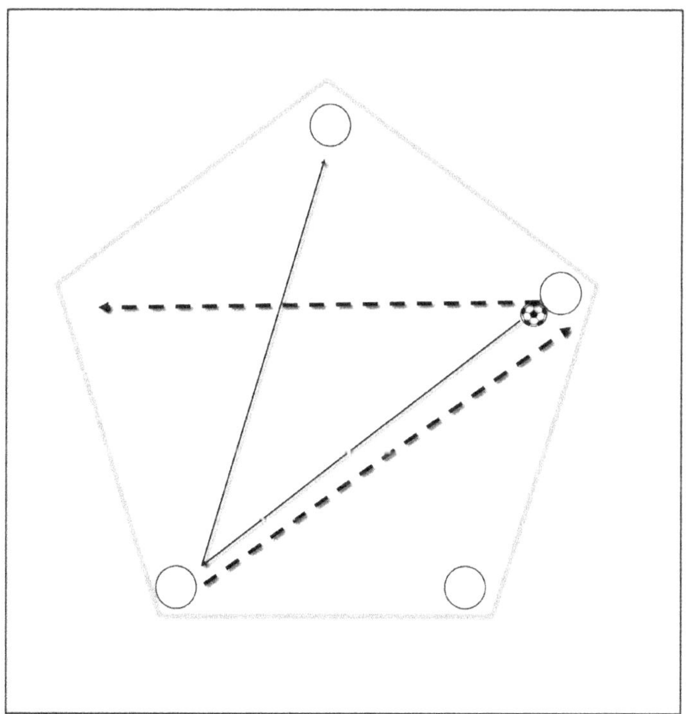

Drill N° 14	Main Objective	Pass improvement
	Number of players	5

Explanation

Players as shown in the picture. Players pass by and they're going to take the free side. Players must be well profiled always and in a position to receive.

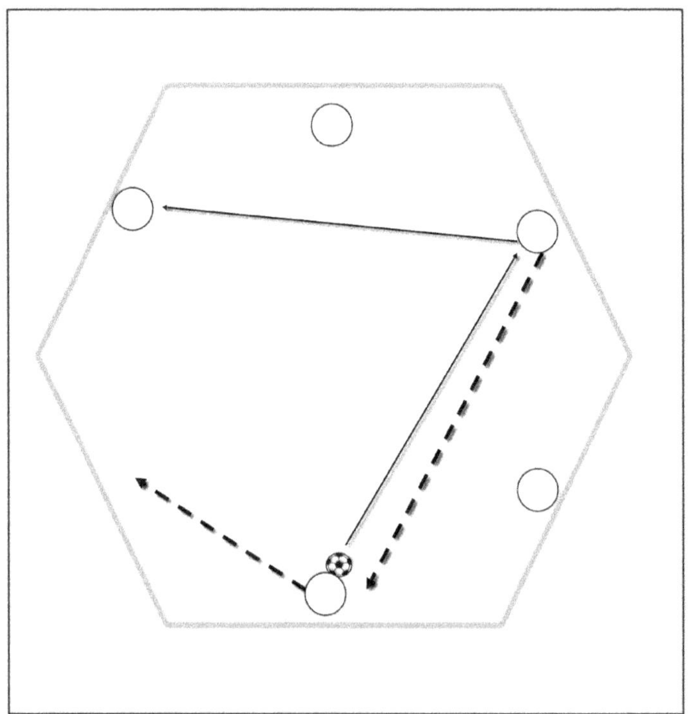

Drill N° 15	Main Objective	Pass improvement
	Number of players	3 (2x1)

Explanation

Players as shown in the picture. They will pass the ball between them and in the center a player will try to intercept the pass and move sideways in the aisle.

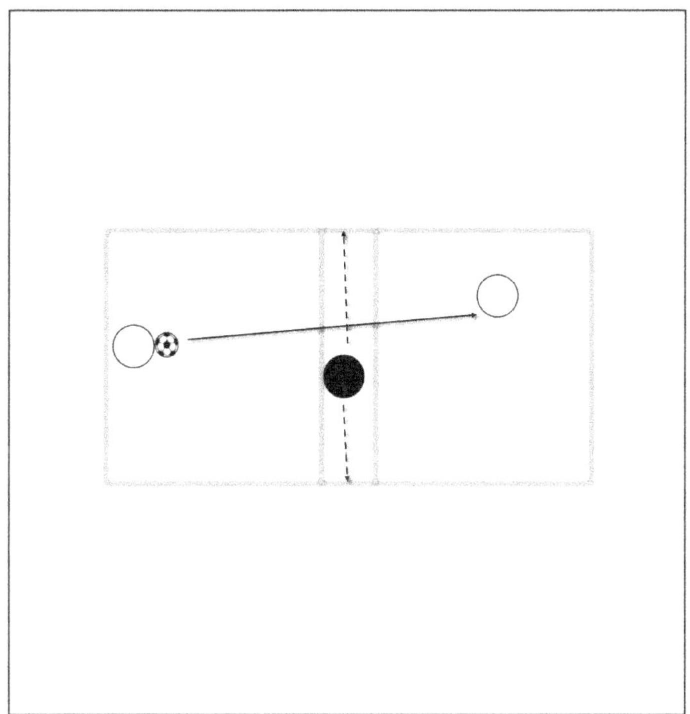

Drill N°16	Main Objective	Pass improvement
	Number of players	3 (2x1)

Explanation

Players as shown in the picture. They will pass the ball to the teammate on the other side, when the aisle player enters his square to steal. If the player in the hallway steals the ball, roles are changed.

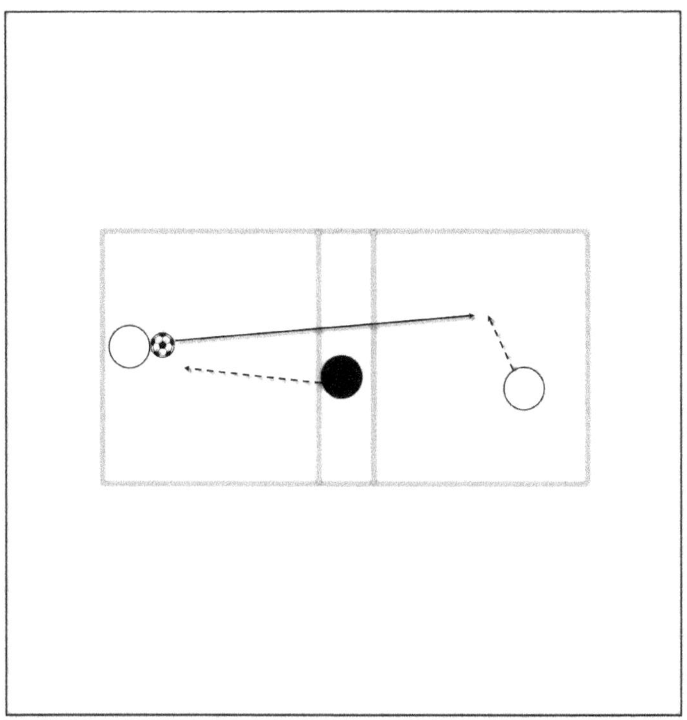

Drill N° 17	Main Objective	Pass improvement
	Number of players	4 (2x2)

Explanation

Players as shown in the picture, will pass the ball between them. In the center a rival player will try to intercept the pass, moving side to side in the aisle. Another rival player will press the one he receives. Black players change roles when the ball passes.

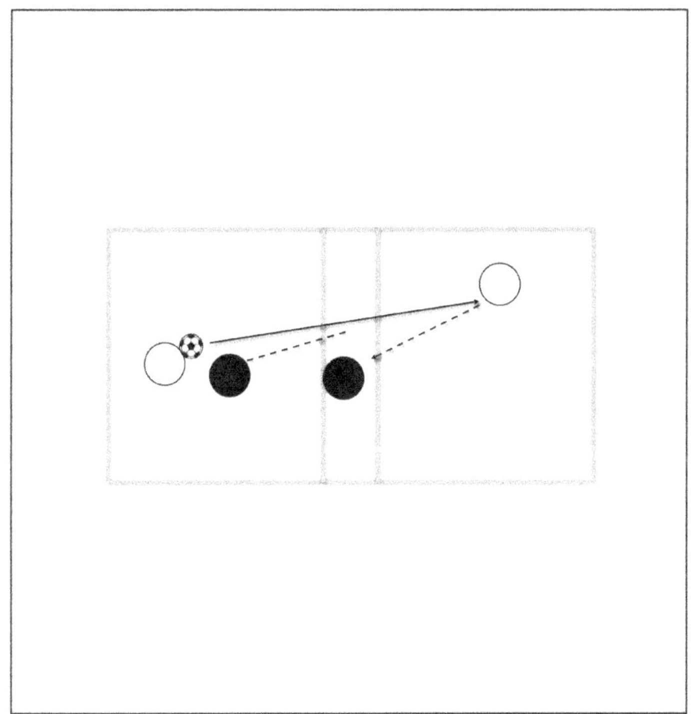

Drill N° 18	Main Objective	Pass improvement
	Number of players	5 (2x3)

Explanation

Players as shown in the picture. The two players pass the ball between them. In the center an opponent will try to intercept the pass moving side to side in the aisle. Two other rivals behind them from the outside, and each will come in to press to the one that receives the ball.

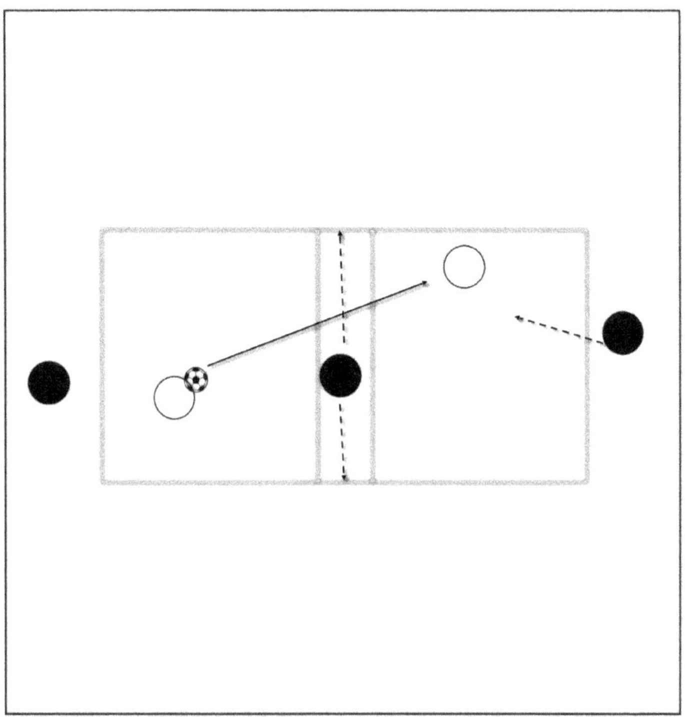

Drill N° 19	Main Objective	Pass improvement
	Number of players	3

Explanation

Players as shown in the picture. They pass the ball between them. In the center a player will attempt to intercept the pass moving side to side in the aisle. Player number 3 will have to go to the aisle to receive and return the ball to 2.

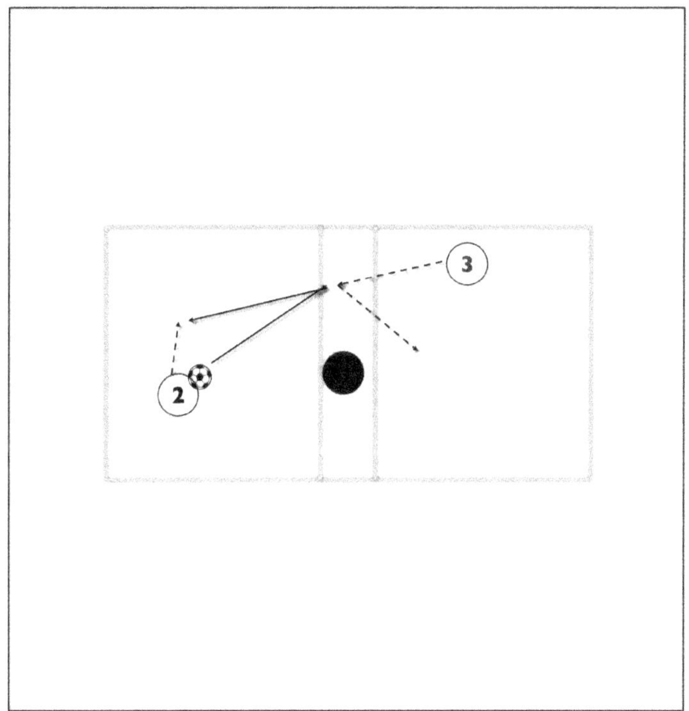

Drill N° 20	Main Objective	Pass improvement
	Number of players	4 (2x2)

Explanation

Players as shown in the picture. Players on the white team will pass the ball between them. In the center a rival player will attempt to intercept the pass moving side to side in the aisle. Another opposing player will be in the area where the number 3 player is. Player number 3 will have to move to either aisle to receive and return the ball to 2. Player 2 will only be able to move through the center aisle, or through its initial zone.

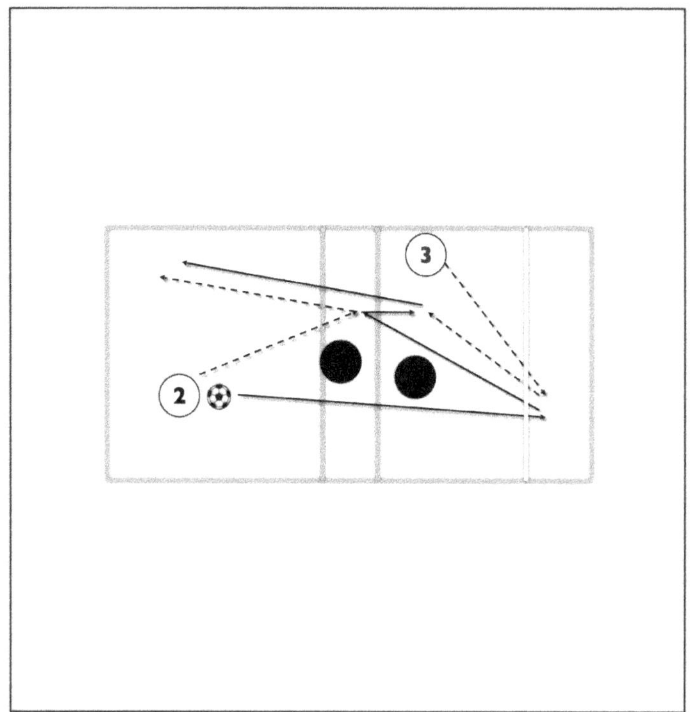

Drill N° 21	Main Objective	Pass improvement
	Number of players	9 (2x1+6)

Explanation

Players as shown in the picture. They'll pass the ball between them. In the center, a rival player will attempt to intercept the pass moving side to side in the aisle. The other six opposing players will only enter to try to anticipate the reception, but will not be able to press.

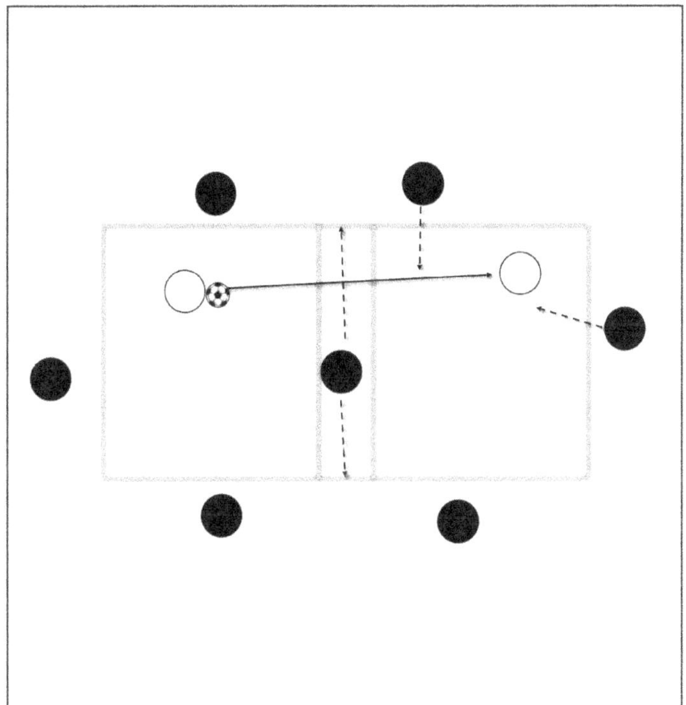

Drill N° 22	Main Objective	Pass improvement
	Number of players	5 (2x3)

Explanation

Players as shown in the picture. They pass the ball between them. In the center, a rival player will attempt to intercept the pass, moving side to side in the aisle and can also swap positions with the other two black players who are in one of the zones. Players who are passing the ball will move, to receive, to the space left free by the defenders. Defenders may change areas only before the pass occurs, but they will be able to intercept at all times within their zone.

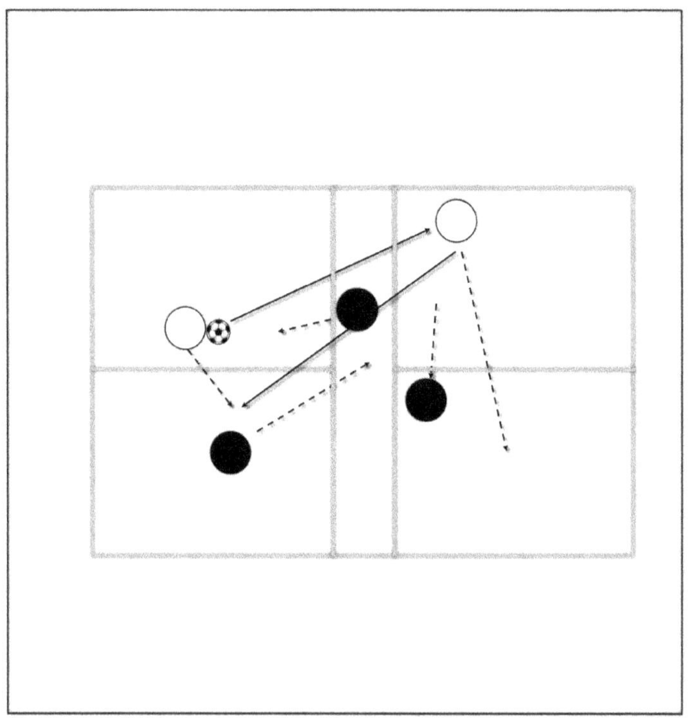

Drill N° 23	Main Objective	Pass improvement
	Number of players	7(4x3)

Explanation

Players as shown in the picture. They pass the ball between them. In the center, rival players, each in a corridor, will try to intercept the pass, being able to move sideways in their aisle.

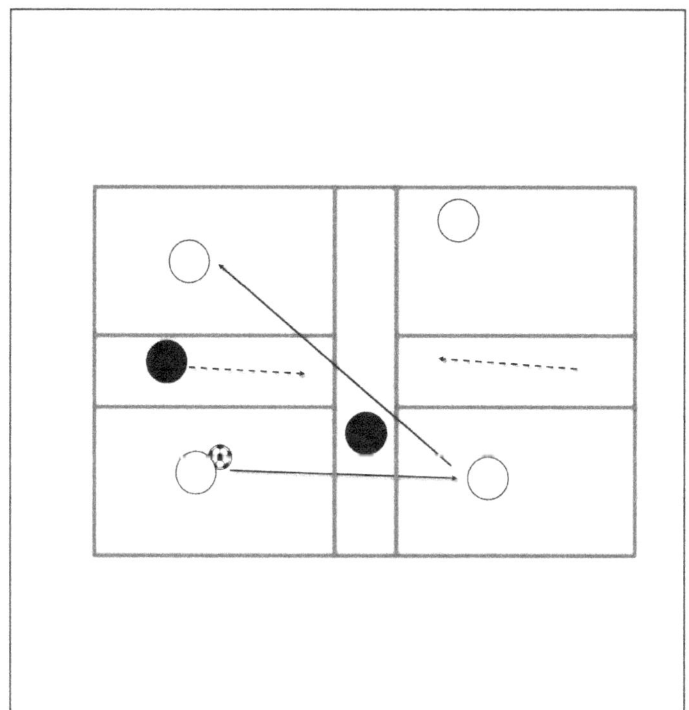

Drill N° 24	Main Objective	Pass improvement
	Number of players	7(4x3)

Explanation

Players as shown in the picture. White players pass the ball between them. In the center, rival players, each in a corridor, will attempt to intercept the pass, moving side to side in their aisle, and can also enter to press the areas of the players of the white team.

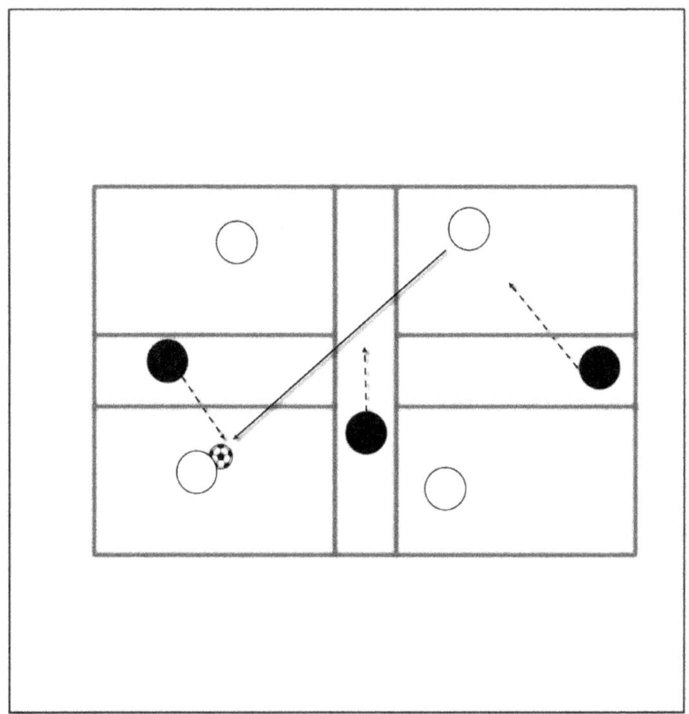

Drill N° 25	Main Objective	Pass improvement
	Number of players	7 (4x3)

Explanation

Players distributed as shown in the picture. White players pass the ball, having a free player in a square. The white player who has the ball will receive pressure from a black player, always leaving a white partner free in a square.

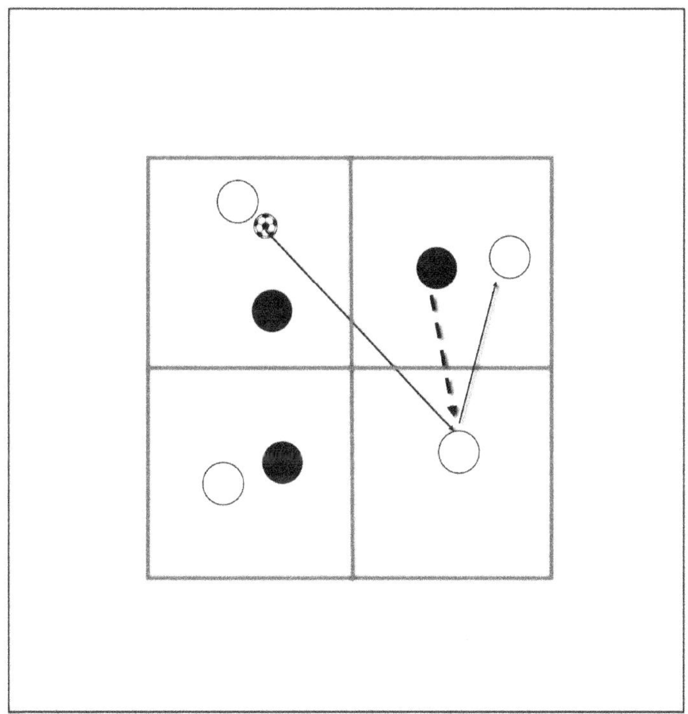

Drill N° 26	Main Objective	Pass improvement
	Number of players	20

Explanation

Within the area, players pass the ball in pairs. Two pairs pass the ball from the sides, trying to get the ball to the partner on the other side, without touching either the rest of the balls or the rest of the players inside the rectangle. If the ball touches on one of those inside, the two teams change their roles.

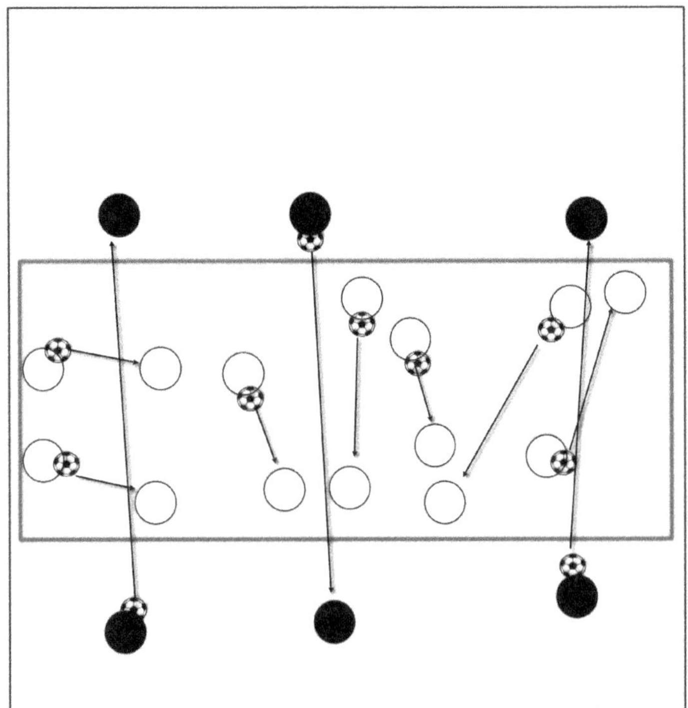

Drill Nº 27	Main Objective	Pass improvement
	Number of players	13

Explanation

Players pass on to the teammate who is in front of them, and three players try to intercept. The one who intercepts, changes his role with the one who made the wrong pass.

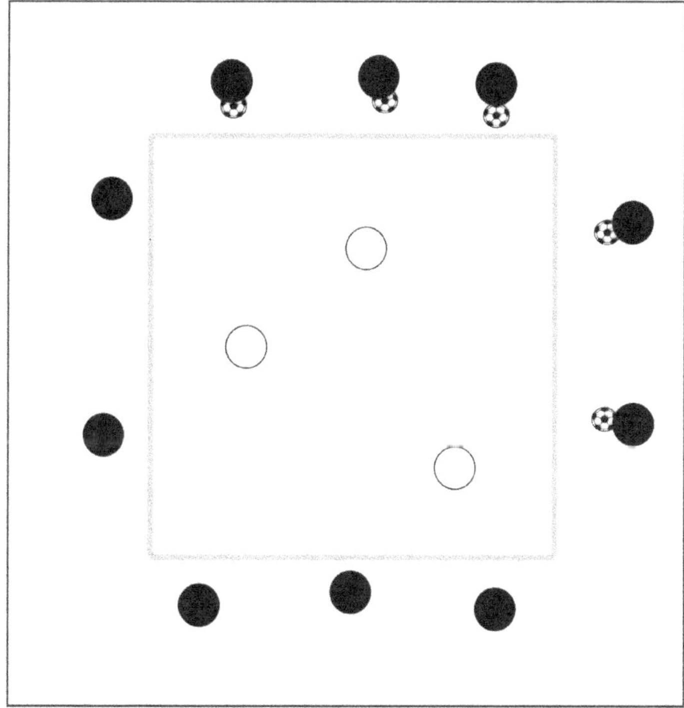

Drill N° 28	Main Objective	Pass improvement
	Number of players	22

Explanation

Within a rectangle, players pass the ball in pairs. 10 players on the outside, around the rectangle, who can only enter to intercept the passes, but will not be able to enter to press. The player who intercepts will change the role who made the wrong pass.

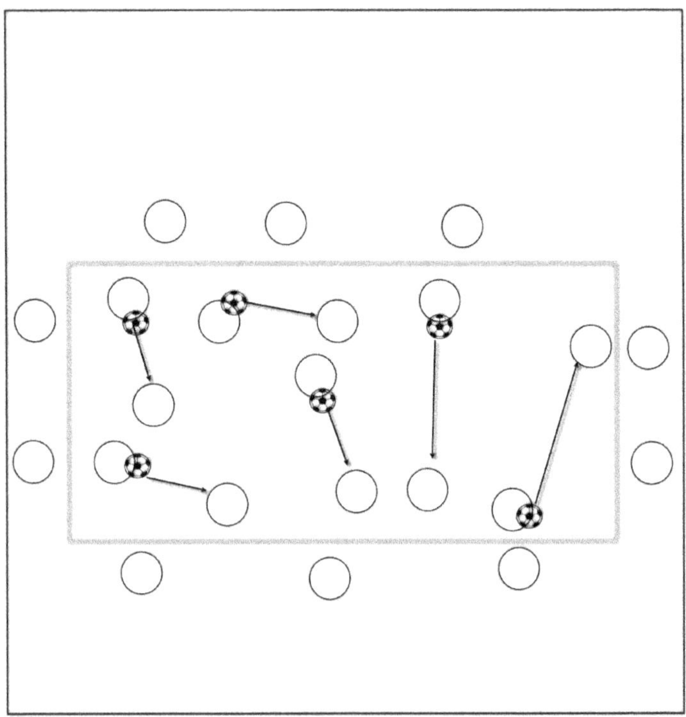

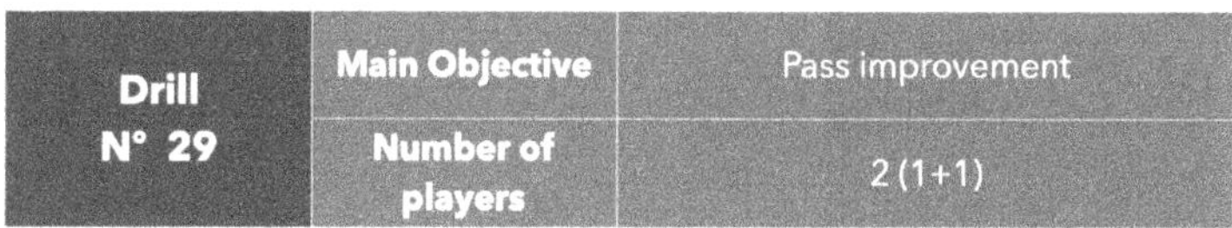

Drill N° 29	Main Objective	Pass improvement
	Number of players	2 (1+1)

Explanation

The player who has no ball moves to one of the cones. And the one with the ball passes the ball to the cone to which the other is headed.

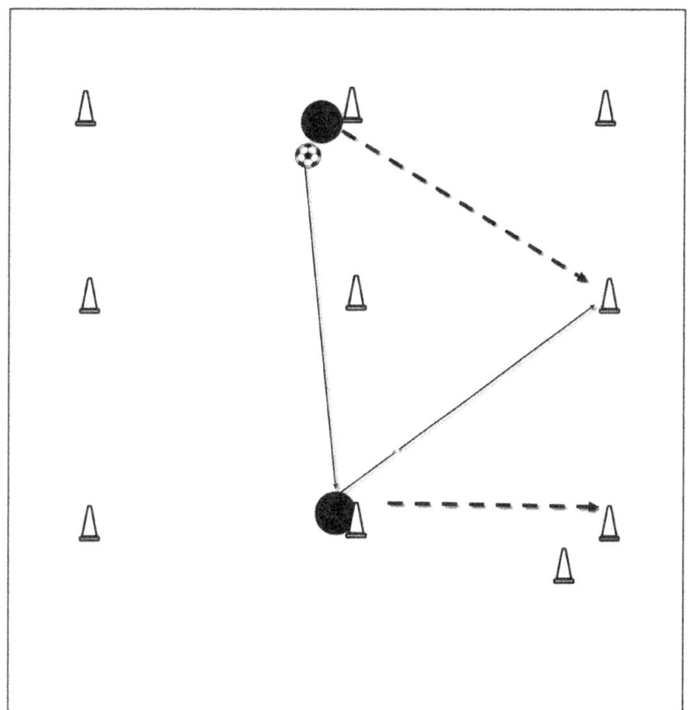

Drill N° 30	Main Objective	Driving ball improvement
	Number of players	2

Explanation

Players driving the ball to the cone of center. Whoever arrives first, goes to one side, and the other has to go to the opposite side.

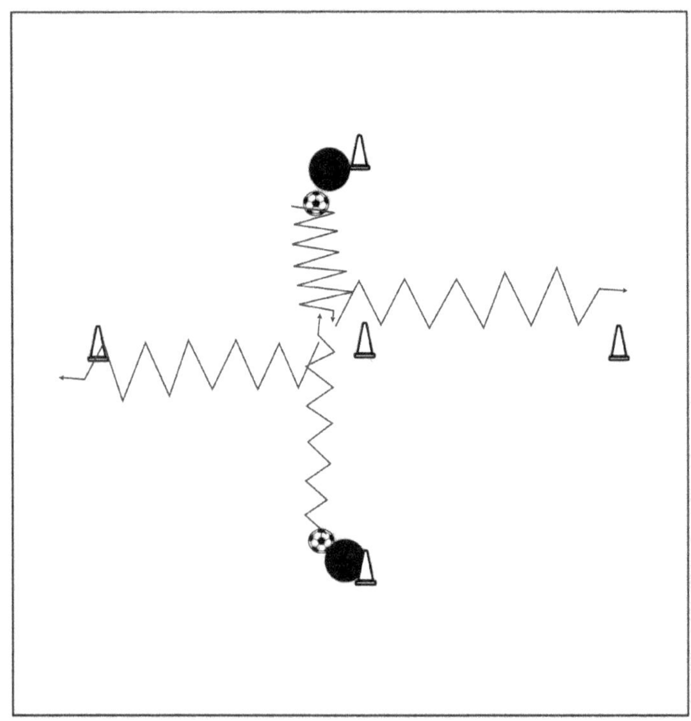

Drill N° 31	Main Objective	Driving ball improvement
	Number of players	2

Explanation

Players go to the cone of the center, one driving the ball and the other without a ball. The player without the ball decides to go to one side, and the player with the ball will have to go to the opposite side.

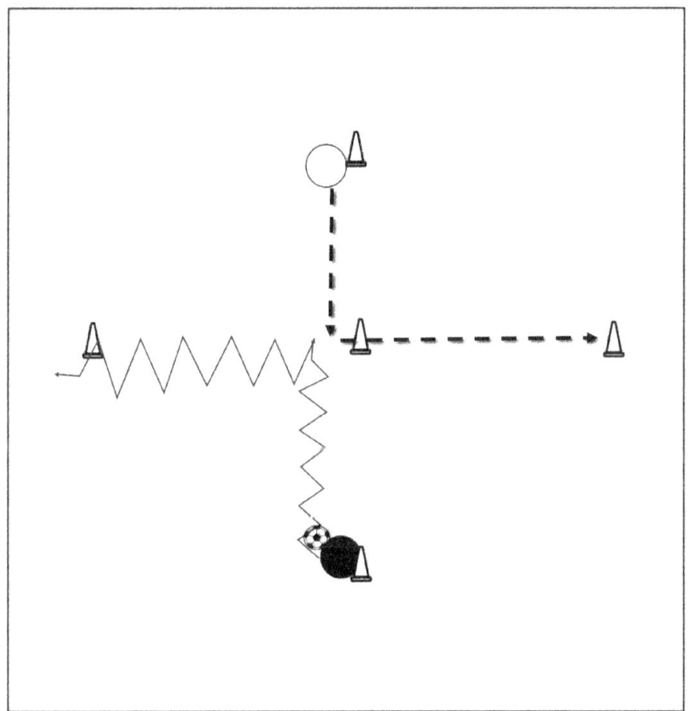

Drill N° 32	Main Objective	Driving ball improvement
	Number of players	4

Explanation

Players driving ball towards the cone of the center. And then, each of them, has to go to a cone that wasn't busy at the beginning.

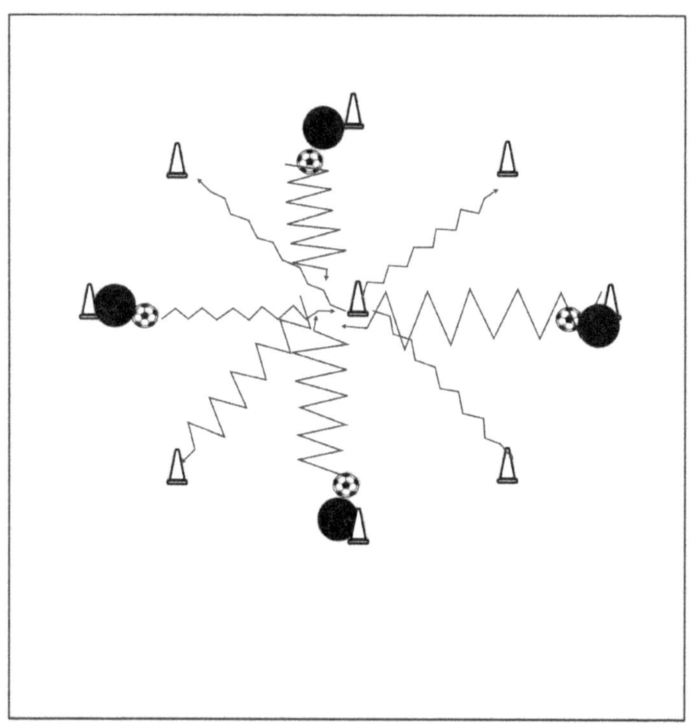

Drill N° 33	Main Objective	Driving ball improvement
	Number of players	3

Explanation

Players drive through the corridors. The rule is that no more than one player can coincide within the same box.

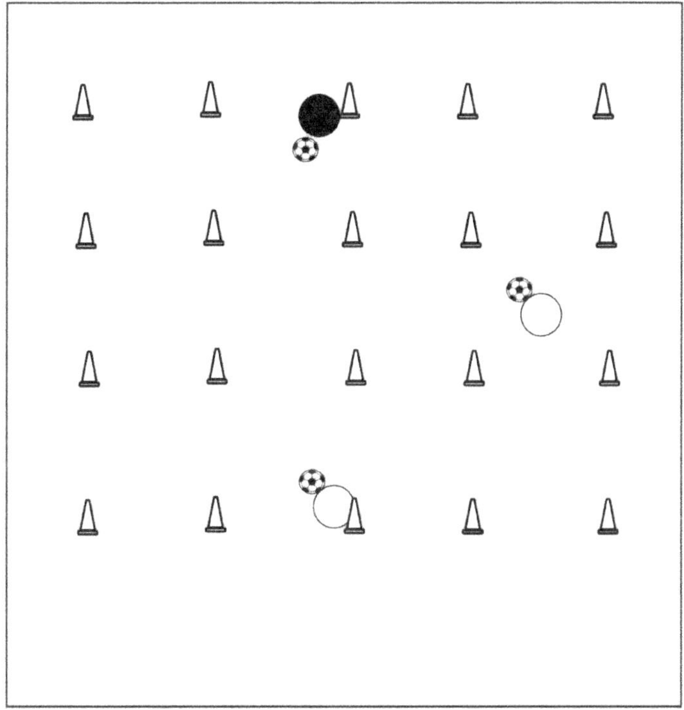

Drill N° 34	Main Objective	Driving ball improvement
	Number of players	12

Explanation

10 players drive the ball inside the square, dodging the other players. And there will be two players without a ball, pulling out of the square the balls of the other players. When a player loses the ball, he will have to go after him, and get back inside by driving.

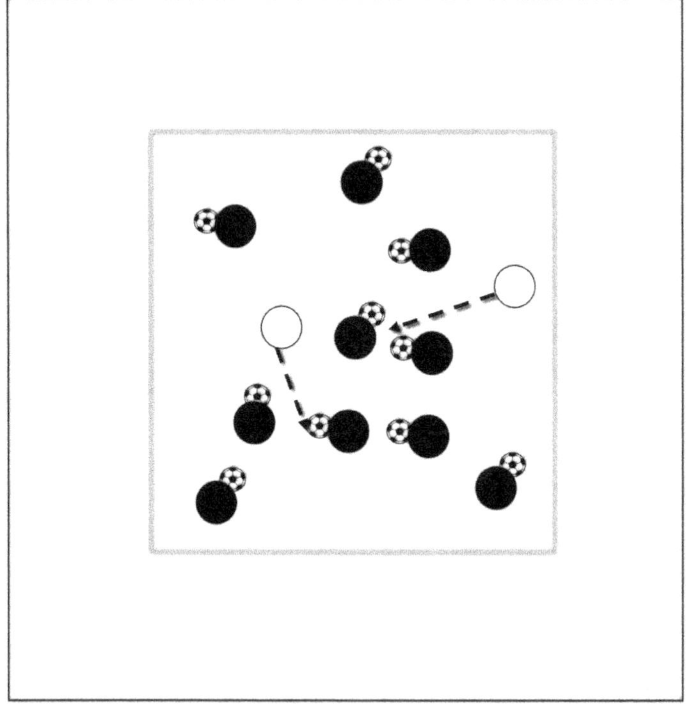

Drill N° 35	Main Objective	Driving ball improvement
	Number of players	12

Explanation

10 players drive the ball inside the square dodging the other players. And there will be two players trying to take the ball from them. The player who loses the ball will change the role with the player who stole it.

Drill N° 26	Main Objective	Shot improvement
	Number of players	2 (1xP)

Explanation

The goalkeeper, at the penalty spot, passes the ball to the player and goes to one of the goalposts. The player who goes to the cone, must shoot at goal to score.

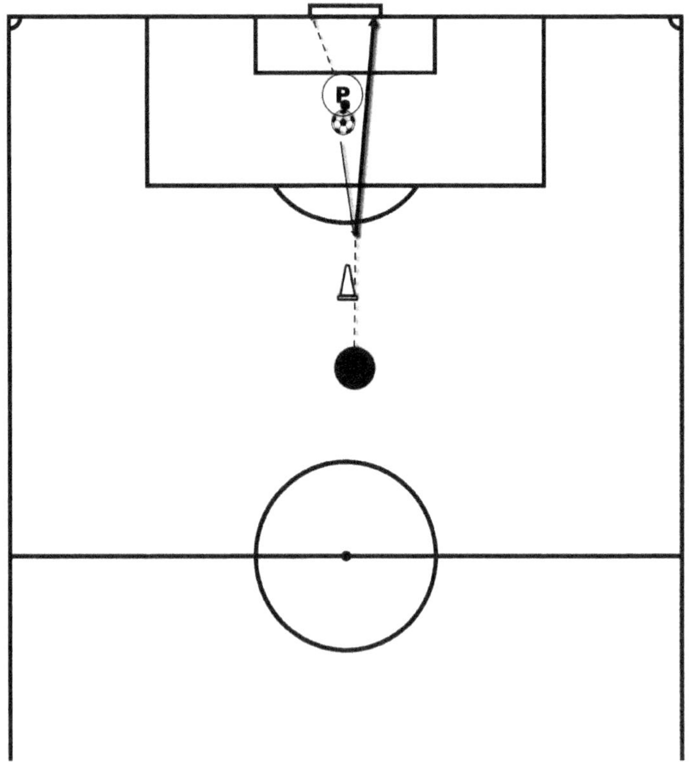

Drill N° 37	Main Objective	Shot improvement
	Number of players	5 (2x2+P)

Explanation

Two players pass the ball between them, without the ball falling to the ground. Two other players come in to press, steal the ball, and go out to shoot with the pressure of those who lost the ball.

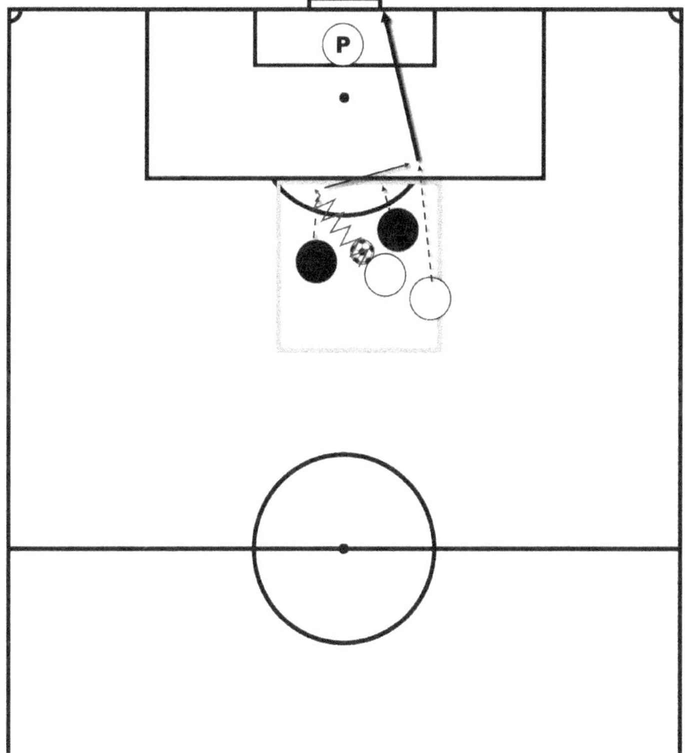

Drill N° 38	Main Objective	Shot improvement
	Number of players	2 (1xP)

Explanation

Each goalkeeper is behind a goal, and passes the ball to the player in front of him. Then he goes to the goal. The player who receives, must shot at goal to score.

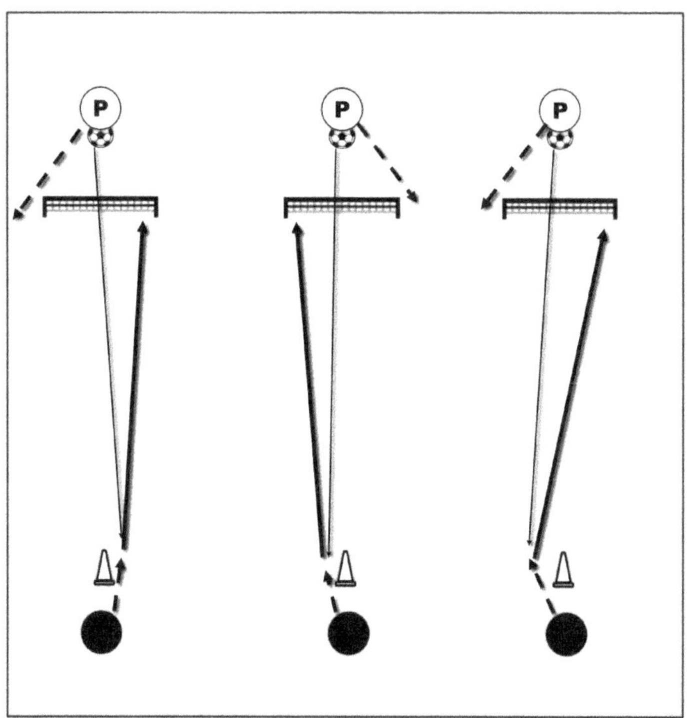

Drill N° 39	Main Objective	Shot improvement
	Number of players	2 (1xP)

Explanation

The goalkeeper passes the ball to the black player, who will attempt to overtake the white player, control the ball and shoot to goal. The white player will press to avoid it. But the white player will be on his back to the black player, and can only react and move when he sees the black player pass by the side.

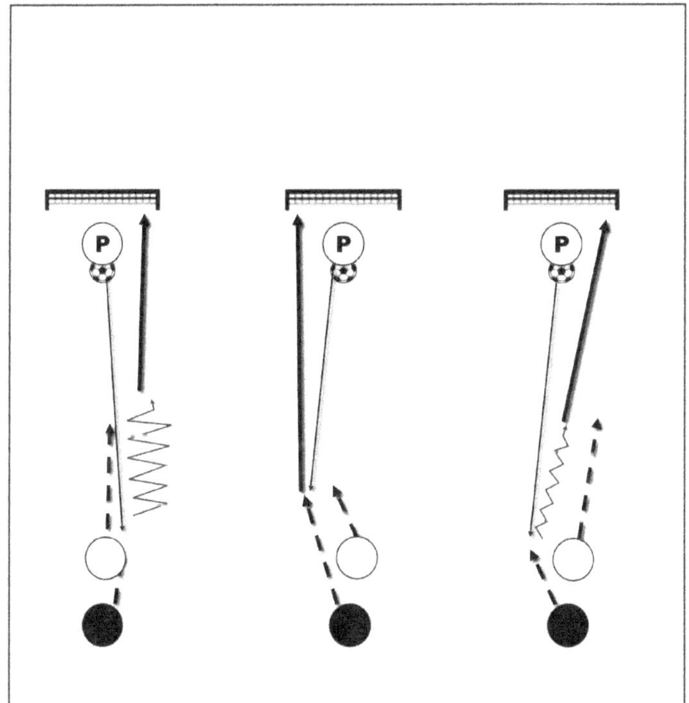

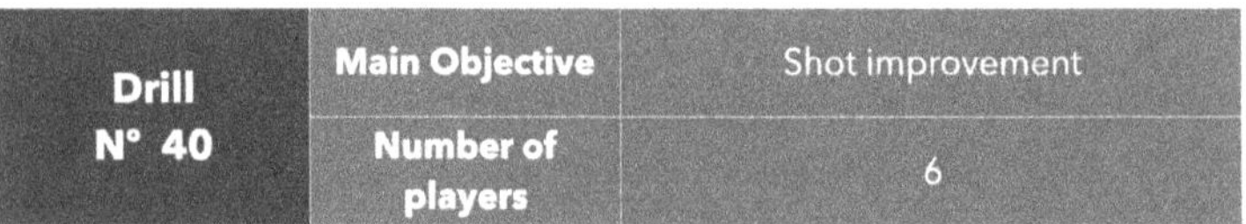

Drill N° 40	Main Objective	Shot improvement
	Number of players	6

Explanation

Players distributed as shown in the picture. Goalkeepers throw the ball in front. Black players receive and attack to shoot at goal. White players defend, and will be able to exit interchangeably towards one or the other player, but coordinating to make the defense one-to-one.

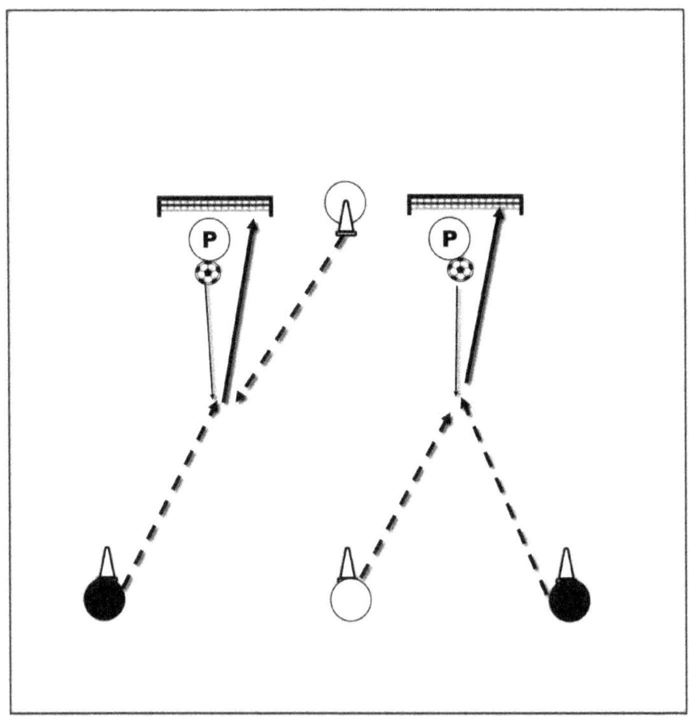

Drill N° 41	Main Objective	Shot improvement
	Number of players	5

Explanation

Players distributed as shown in the picture. Goalkeepers throw the ball in front. The player at the center is a defender. He'll decide which of the two attackers he'll go to, to try to steal the ball.

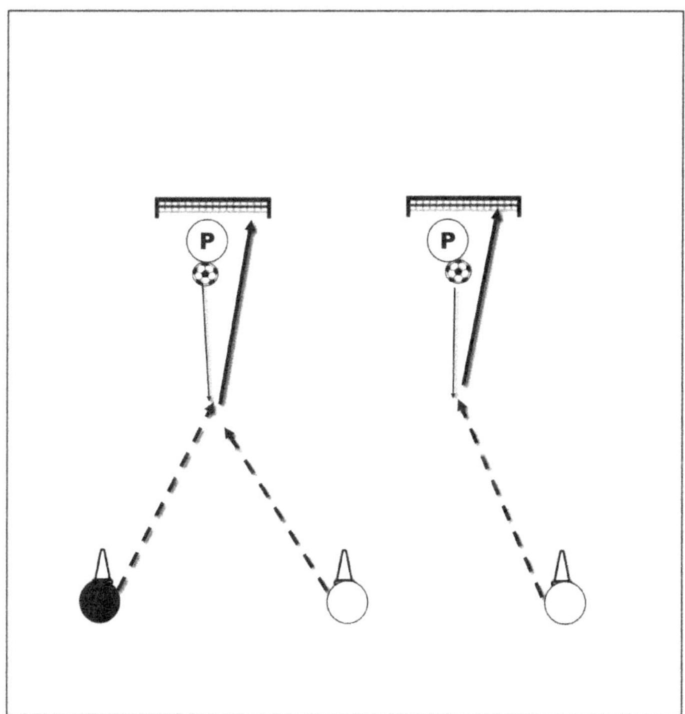

Drill N° 42	Main Objective	Shot improvement
	Number of players	10

Explanation

Players distributed as shown in the picture. Each goalkeeper passes the ball to each (black) attacker, who will receive and attempt to fire at the goal. Of the 4 white defenders only 3 participate who will try to avoid or hinder the shooting at goal. Defenders will alternate their participation. Attackers don't know which defenders are involved or who they're going to put pressure on.

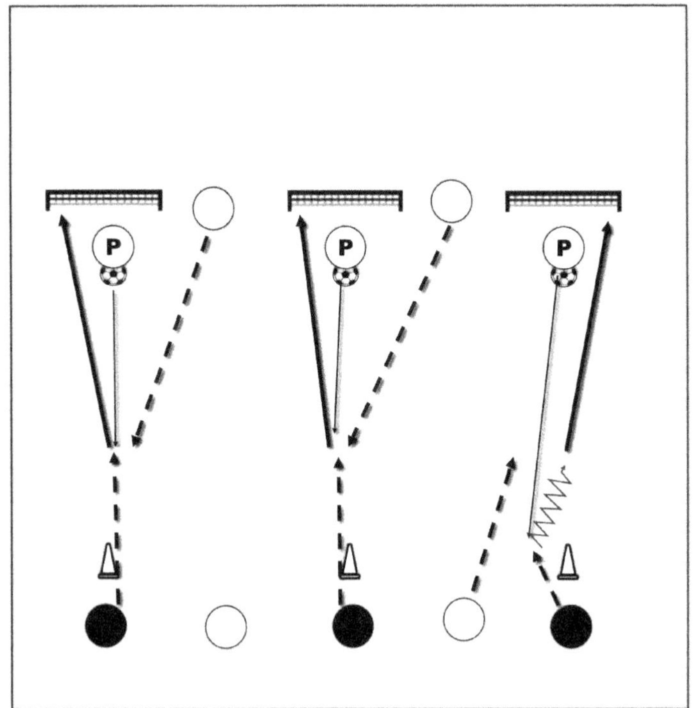

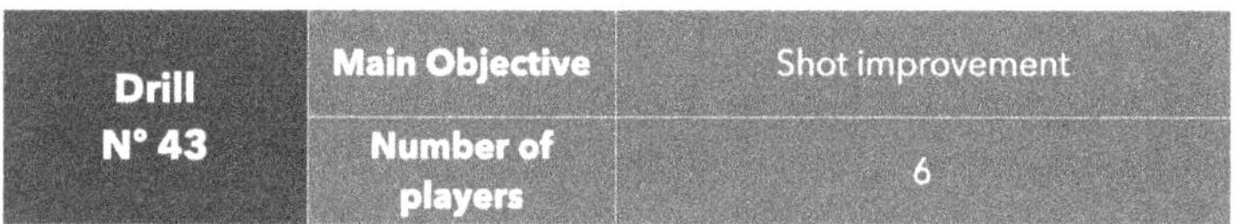

Drill N° 43	Main Objective	Shot improvement
	Number of players	6

Explanation

1 pass to 2. 2 receives and tries to drive the ball and shoot at goal. 3 is a defender, and reacts when 2 pass ball to him. 5 and 6 are defenders, and they press on attacker 2. Player 2 can be leaning on 1 for attack.

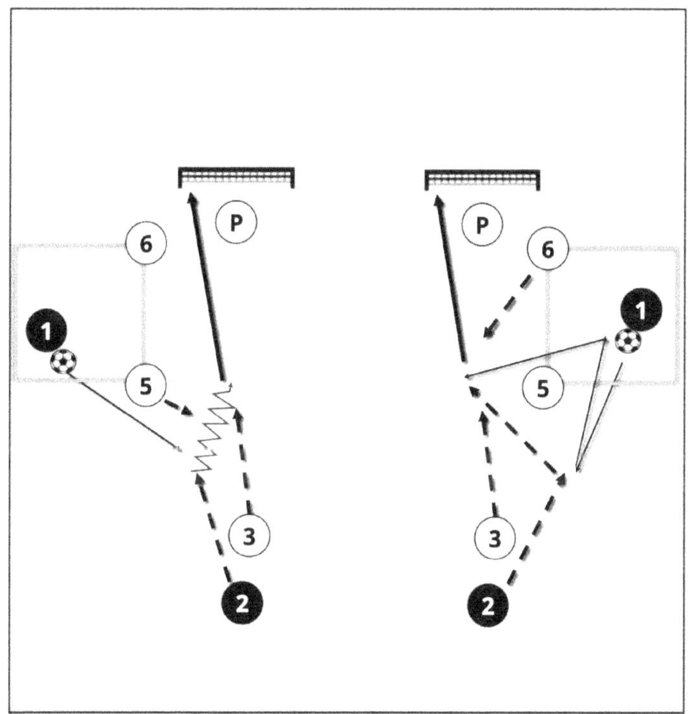

Drill N° 44	Main Objective	Shot improvement
	Number of players	4 (1x3P)

Explanation

The player and goalkeepers distributed as shown in the picture. When the player receives from the goalkeeper he has to turn around and shoot at the goal that has been left empty because the goalkeeper has gone to press. The goalkeepers will change and leave another goal free.

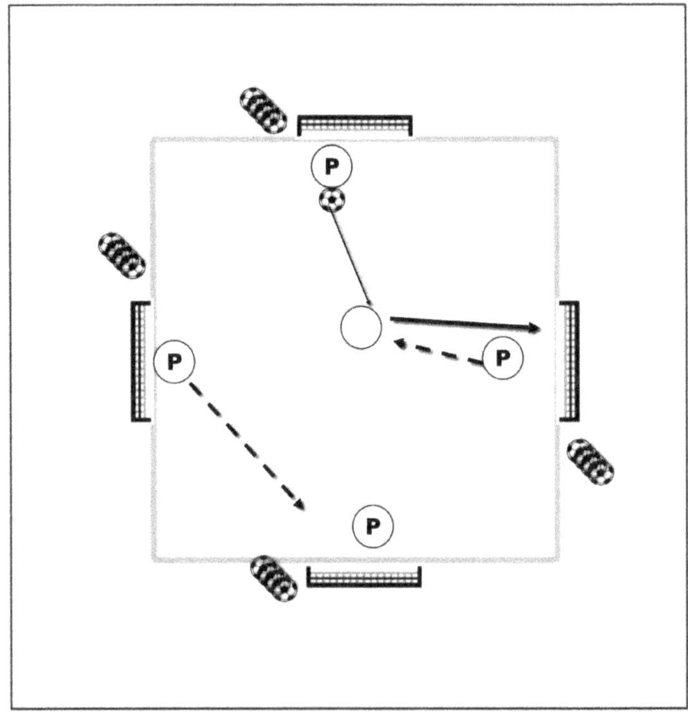

Drill N° 45	Main Objective	Shot improvement
	Number of players	5 (1x4P)

Explanation

The player and goalkeepers distributed as shown in the picture. Three goalkeepers with a ball and one without a ball. One of them will pass the ball to the player, the player will have to orient the body and the ball, to throw to the goal where there is a goalkeeper without a ball. We have to rotate the role of the goalkeepers.

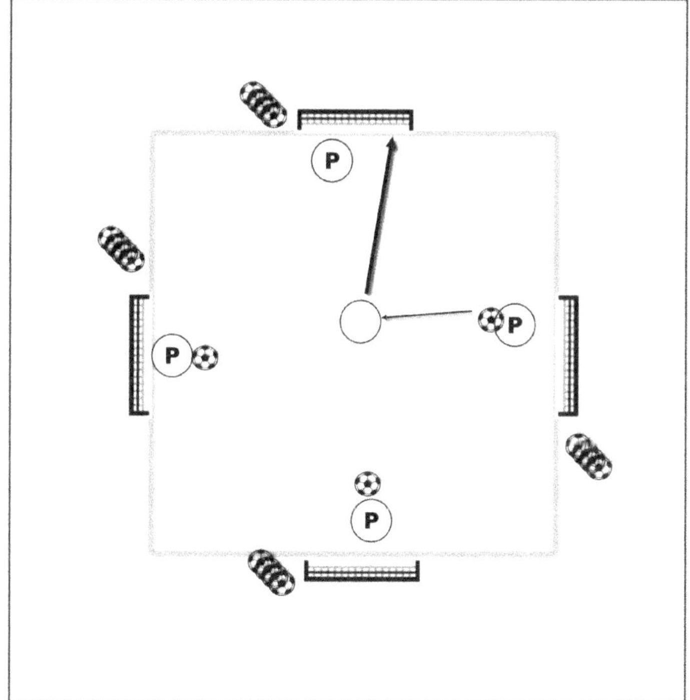

Drill N° 46	Main Objective	Shot improvement
	Number of players	5 (1x2+2P)

Explanation

Players distributed as shown in the picture. When the player receives from the goalkeeper, he has to turn around and shoot at the other goalkeeper with a goalkeeper. The other two players will come to pressure you. Goalkeepers will rotate their goals with the players.

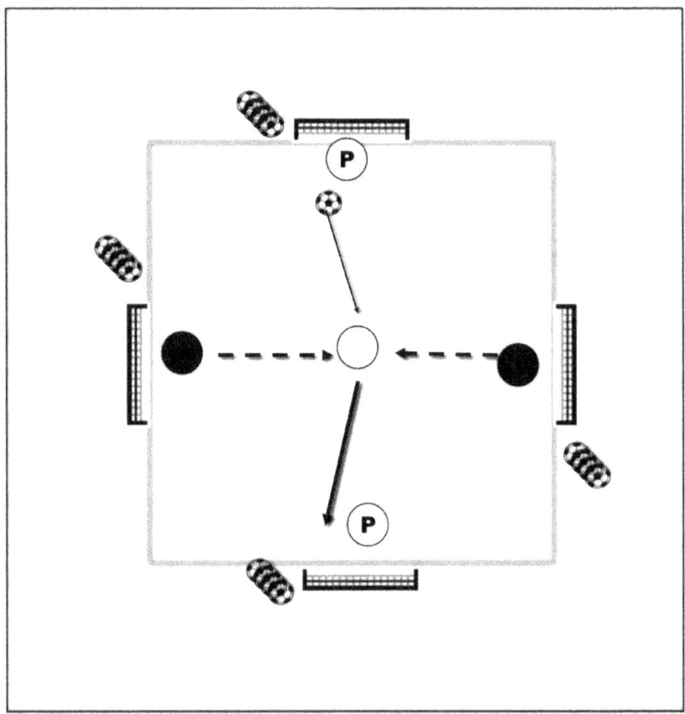

Drill N° 47	Main Objective	Shot improvement
	Number of players	8

Explanation

Players distributed as shown in the picture. When the player receives from the goalkeeper he has to turn around and throw at the other goal he has a goalkeeper. If you want, you can lean on the other two white players in the corners. The two black players are going to put pressure on him. Goalkeepers will rotate their goals with the players.

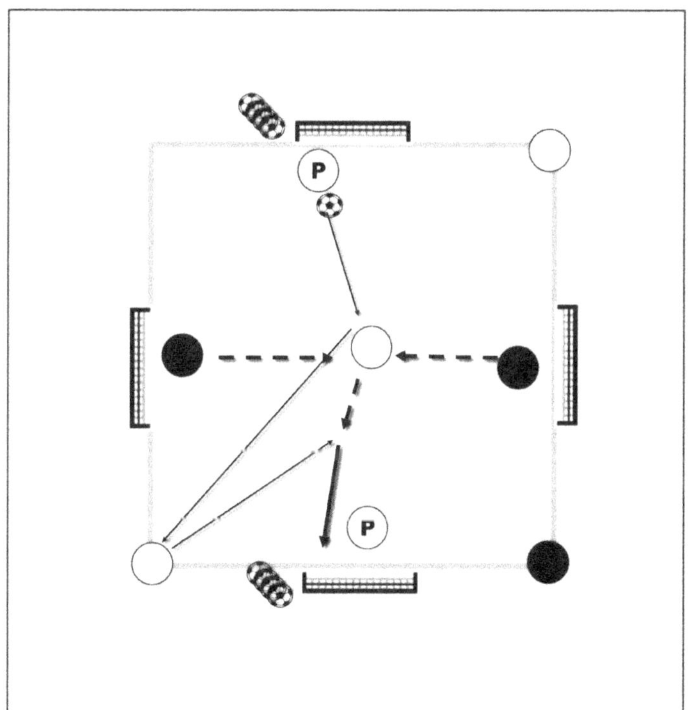

Drill N° 48	Main Objective	Shot improvement
	Number of players	8

Explanation

Players distributed as shown in the picture. The player in the center passes ball to his teammate as in the picture. When opponents enter the field to press, they play with the furthest of them next to the goal. Only two players enter the defending team, and from one repetition of the exercise to another, they will not be the same players or the same sides.

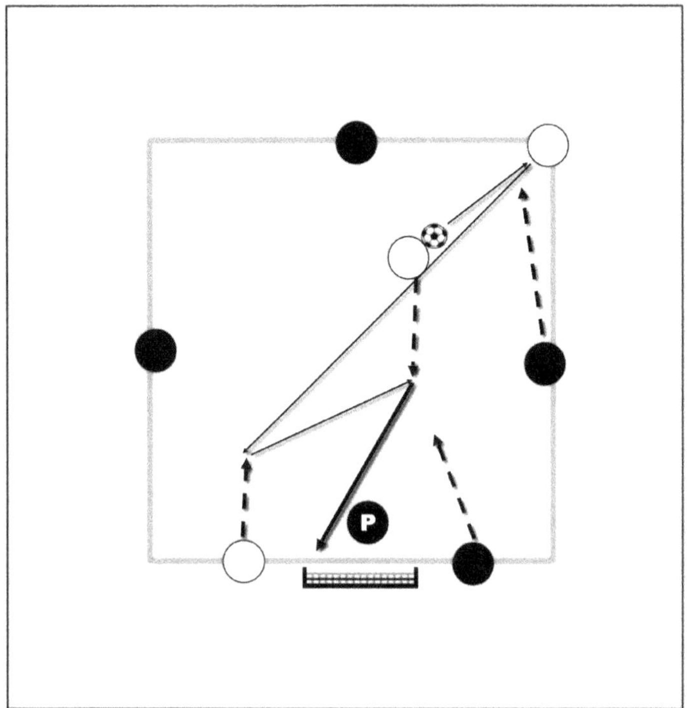

Drill N° 49	Main Objective	Directed first touch
	Number of players	7

Explanation

Players distributed as shown in the picture. When the player from the center receives from the teammate, he has to do directed first touch by pulling the ball out of the square, away from the range of the two players who will press him, and will pass to the other teammate. You have to alternate who are the two players who will to press, and who is the player who will receive.

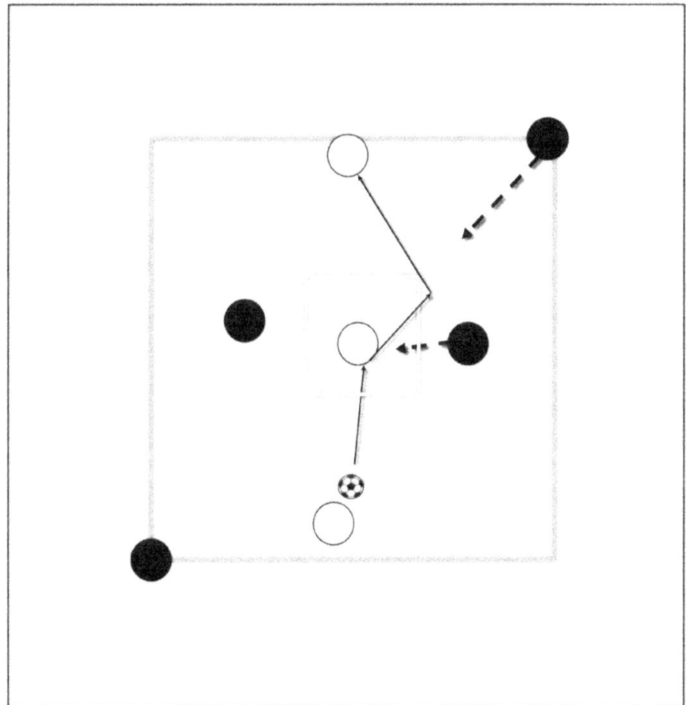

Drill N° 50	Main Objective	Directed first touch
	Number of players	5 (1+1+1x2)

Explanation

Players distributed as shown in the picture. 1 passes ball to 2. Two players (4 and 5) come out to press. 2 makes directed first touch, and has to pass to the only player who has not gone to press those who have the ball (3). The pass of 2 always inside the square, the reception always outside the square. Players from outside will switch between them the roles of pressing or waiting for the pass. 2 doesn't know which players are going to pressure him, he has to visualize the action while he gets the ball.

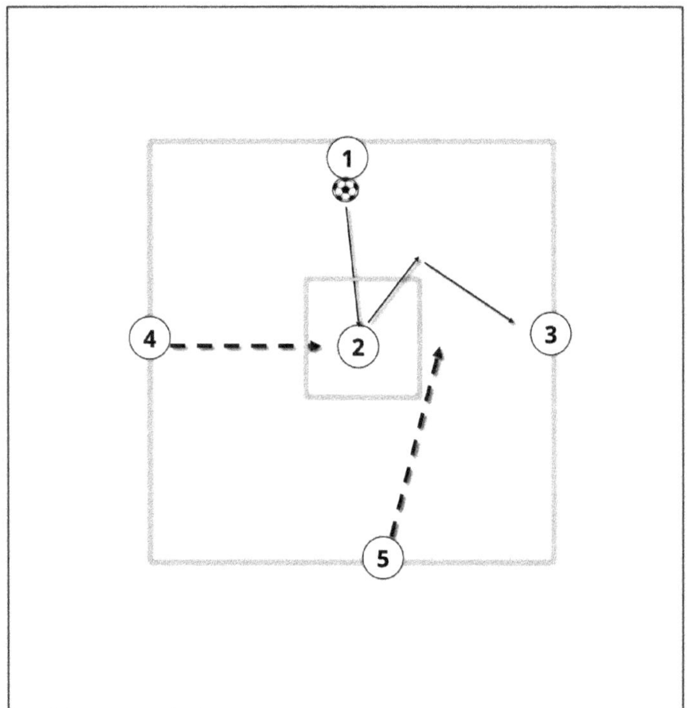

Drill N° 51	Main Objective	Directed first touch and shot
	Number of players	4 (1x3P)

Explanation

The player and goalkeepers distributed as shown in the picture. When the player receives from the goalkeeper, he has to make directed first touch, pull the ball out of the square, and throw at the goal from which he was not pressed and therefore still has a goalkeeper. The goalkeepers will change in each action the ones who will press and those who stay. The idea is that the player does not know in every play what will be the function of each goalkeeper.

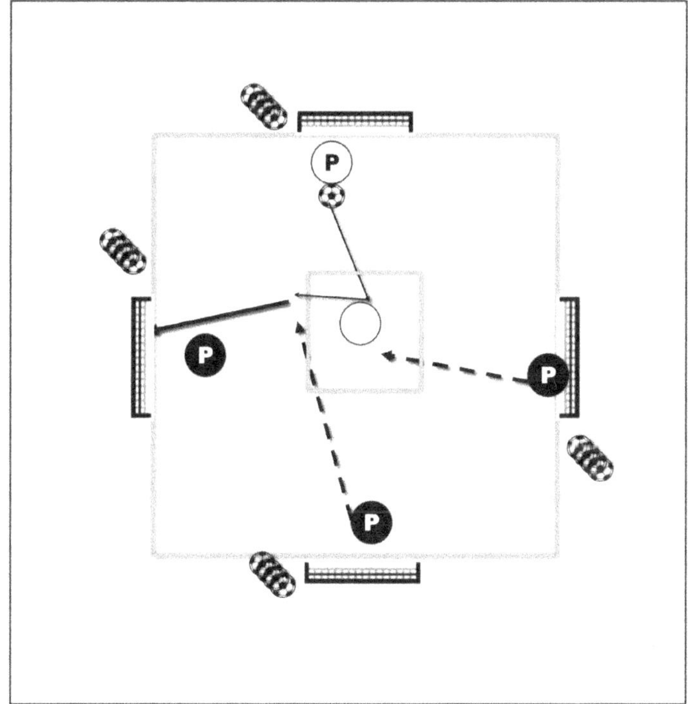

Drill N° 52	Main Objective	Directed first touch and shot
	Number of players	7

Explanation

Players distributed as shown in the picture. When the player receives from the goalkeeper he has to do a directed first touch, taking the ball out of the square, and shoot the other goal that has a goalkeeper. Two players press the player with the ball, but can only do so within the square. They will vary goalkeepers, and role of players who press the player with ball.

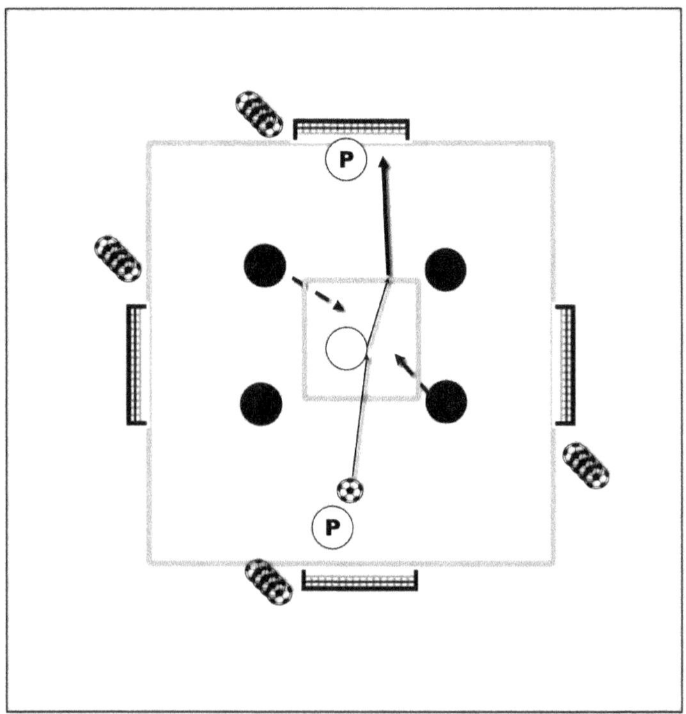

Drill N° 53	Main Objective	Pressing just after lossing the ball
	Number of players	3

Explanation

Players are doing ball mastery, and when one ball is dropped or the ball goes out of the square, the others players will press to steal it.

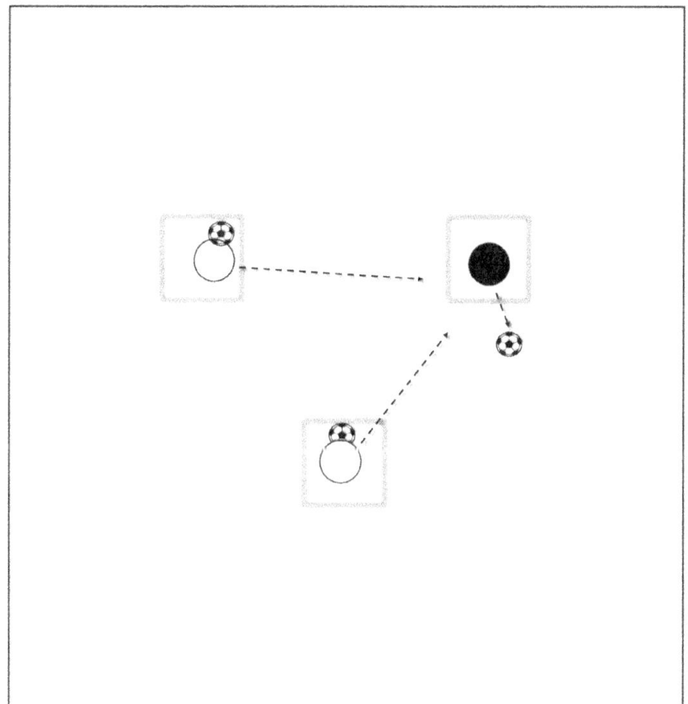

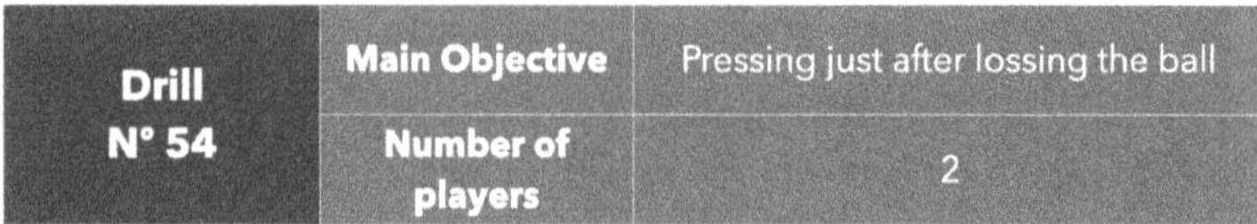

Drill N° 54	Main Objective	Pressing just after lossing the ball
	Number of players	2

Explanation

In pairs. Players are doing ball mastery, and when one ball is dropped or the ball goes out of the square, the other player will press to steal it.

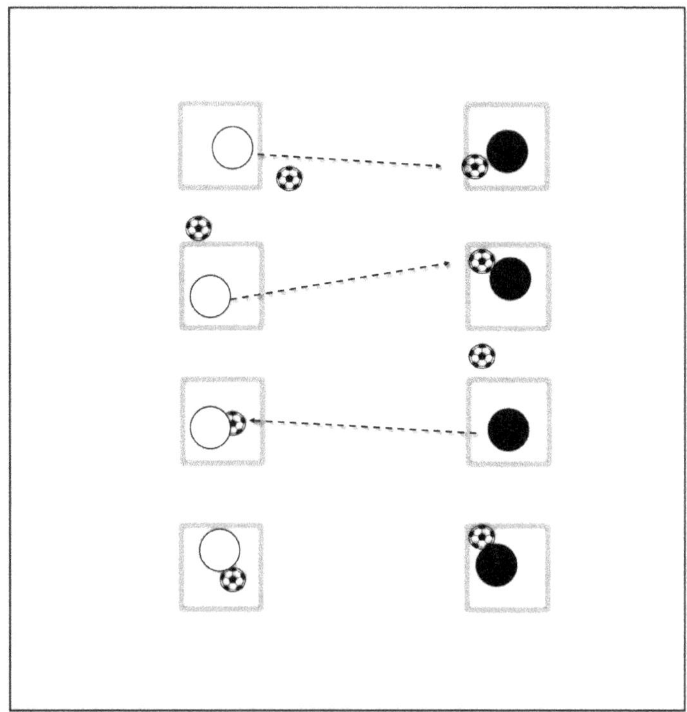

Drill N° 55	Main Objective	Pressing just after lossing the ball
	Number of players	3 (1x1+P)

Explanation

Two players pass the ball without it falling. When the ball comes out of the square, the player who failed will hinder the other's shot.

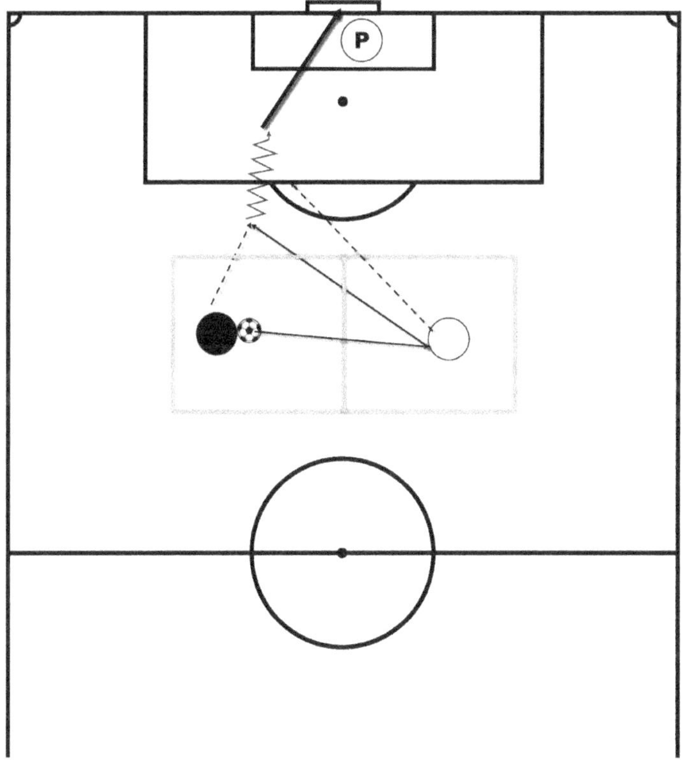

Drill N° 56	Main Objective	Pressing just after lossing the ball
	Number of players	14 (5x5+4)

Explanation

5x5 inside the square. 4 neutral players on the outside of the square. Neutral players will only be able to enter the square to anticipate and, if they steal the ball, move to the other team. Neutral players will always be from the team that doesn't have the ball.

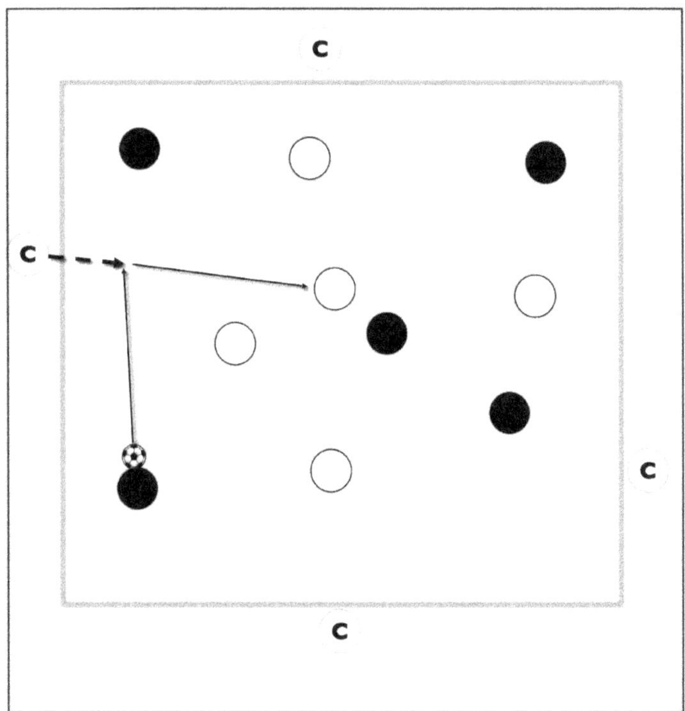

Drill N° 57	Main Objective	Pressing just after lossing the ball
	Number of players	15 (5x5+5)

Explanation

5x5 inside the square. 4 neutral players (c) on the outside of the square, and a neutral player inside the small square. Neutral players will always be from the team that doesn't have the ball, and they will only be able to enter the square to anticipate and move on to the other team.

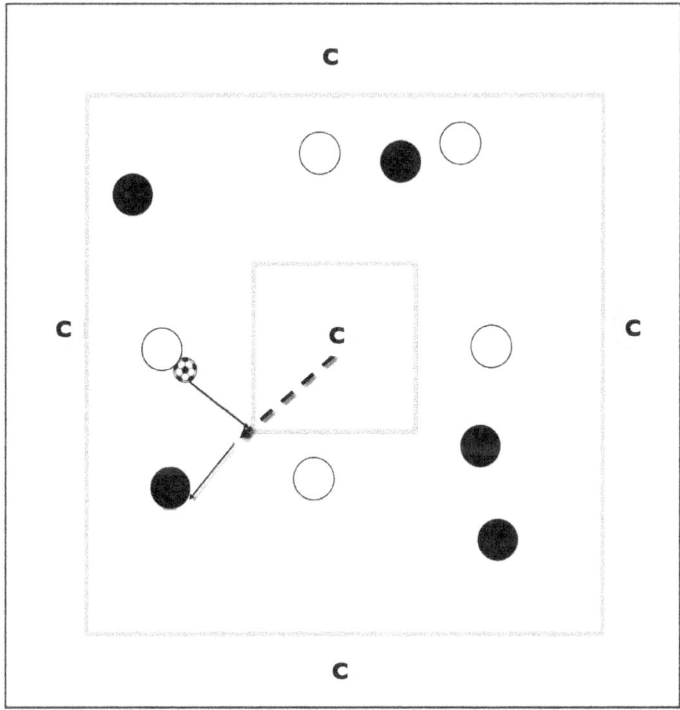

Drill N° 58	Main Objective	Improving the focus of attention during the game
	Number of players	12 (P+2x2+P y P+2x2+P)

Explanation

They play 2 matches simultaneously, one lengthwise and one wide. Players in one match will not be able to touch the ball of the other match, but if they did so inadvertently, they would still play as if the ball had hit a goalpost.

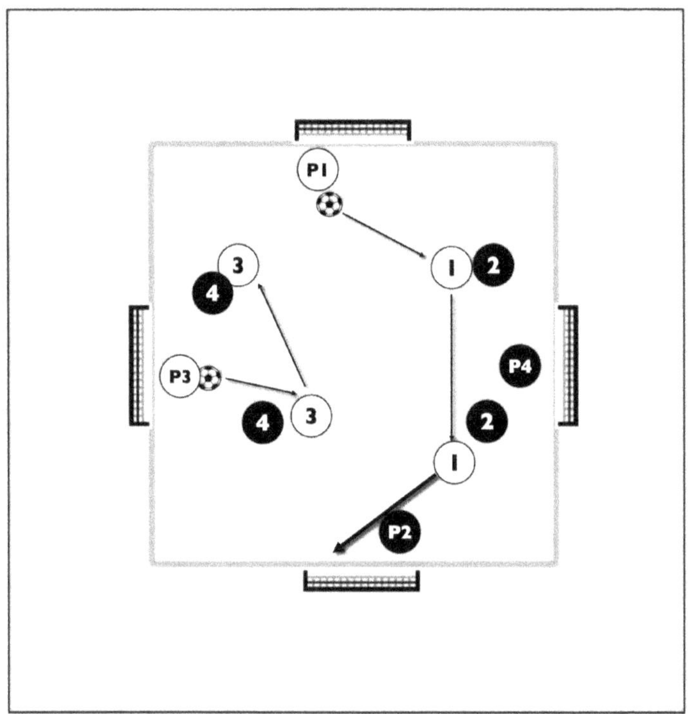

Drill N° 59	Main Objective	Ball possesion improvement
	Number of players	12

Explanation

Players distributed as shown in the picture. The neutral players inside, and the others players over the lines. 2 simultaneous rondos will be played, and players on the center line will participate in the two rondos.

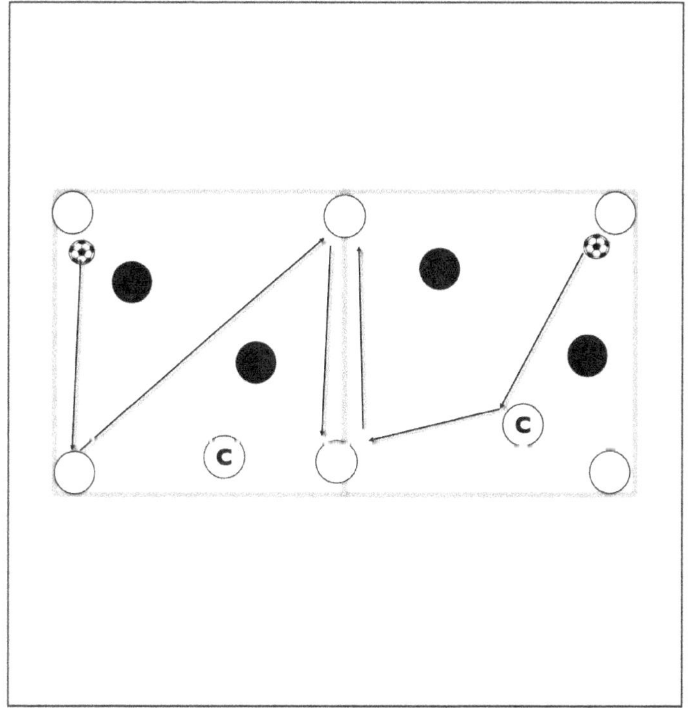

Drill N° 60	Main Objective	Ball possesion improvement
	Number of players	12

Explanation

Players distributed as shown in the picture. Neutral players inside and the other players on the lines. Two simultaneous rondos will be played. Neutral players will participate in the two rondos, and will be able to move, too, around the two rondos.

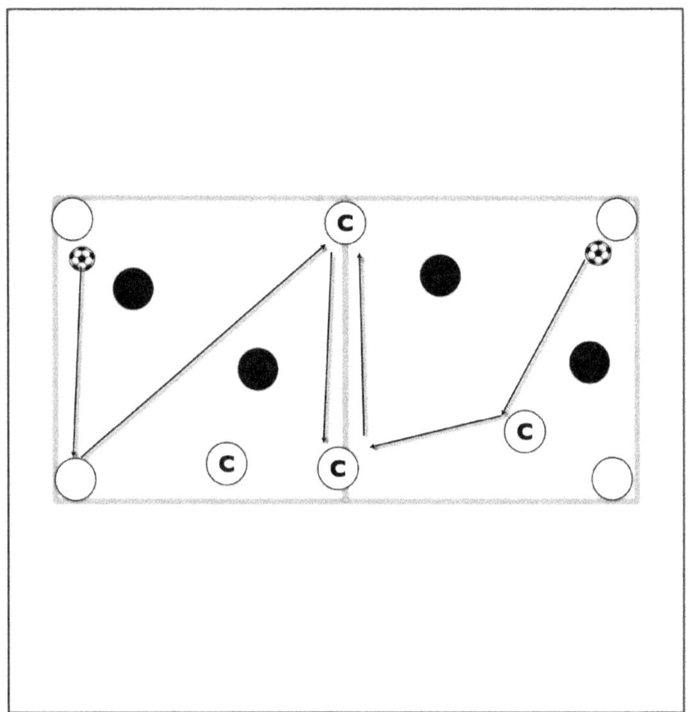

Drill N° 60	Main Objective	Ball possesion improvement
	Number of players	8 (P+3x3+P)

Explanation

The teams, when they lose the ball, retreat to their midfield and divide into the two zones, randomly alternating the defensive structure 2-1, 1-2, 3-0 or 0-3. They can't get out of their zone until they get the ball back, but when they retrieve the ball they will move freely to attack the team that lost the ball. The team that lost the ball will form another defensive structure.

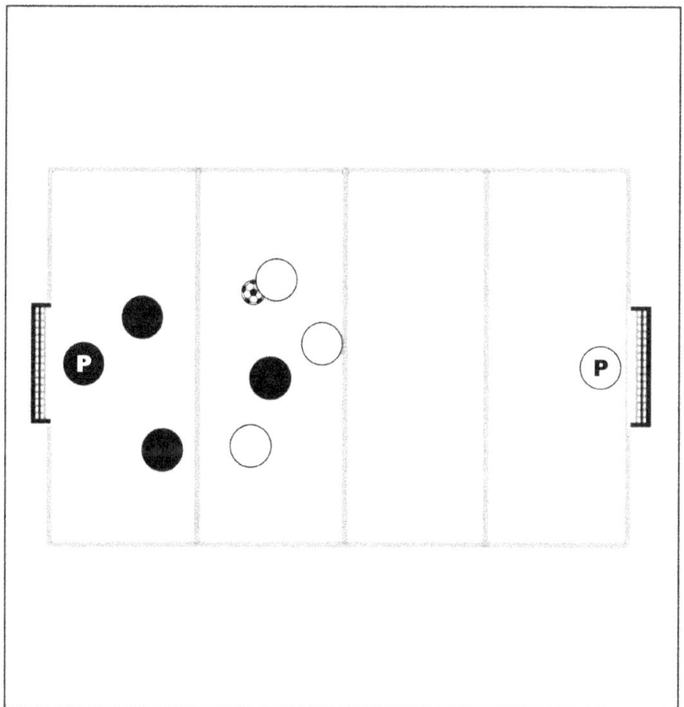

Drill N° 62	Main Objective	Finding spaces in the counterattack
	Number of players	10 (4+Px4+P)

Explanation

4 attackers against four defenders. The attacking team has one player in each side aisle, and two players in the center aisle. The goalkeeper will be on the spot penalty, and will have a ball in his hand. The attacking team will attempt to score by lifting the ball above the goalkeeper. When an attacker shoots at goal, another attacker will have to go to one of the cones behind the goal line, and then return and defend. This movement will leave spaces in the defense of the attacking team, which will now be a defending team. The team that now attacks, will make a counterattack coming out with the ball that the portero had in his hands.

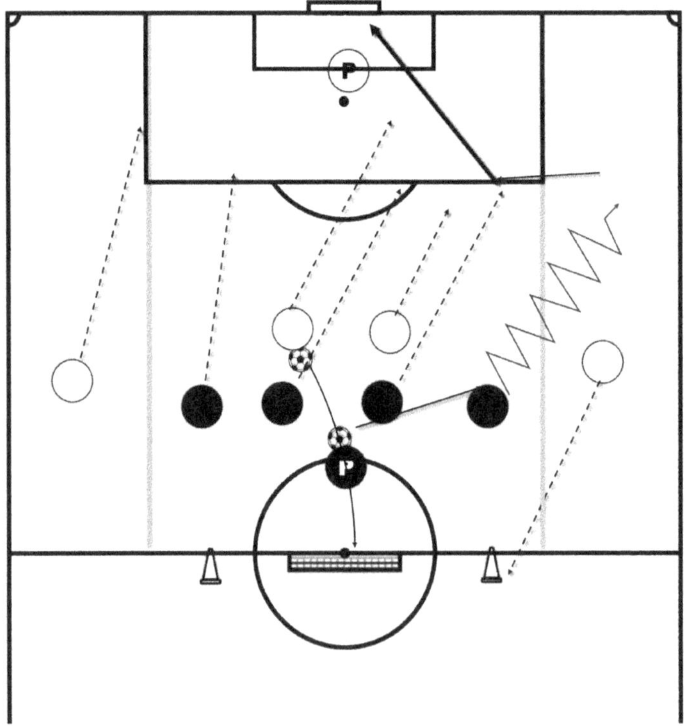

Drill N° 63	Main Objective	Defensive phase of the game
	Number of players	22

Explanation

Match with the split field, as shown in the picture. When the white team loses the ball, he will always perform the same defensive fallback (4-4-2). And the opposing team will change the number of players attacking for each zone (from which they will not be able to leave): 4-3-3, 4-4-2, 3-5-2... The changes of formations will be guided by the trainer. Each time the white team defends, the opponent will have a different formation.

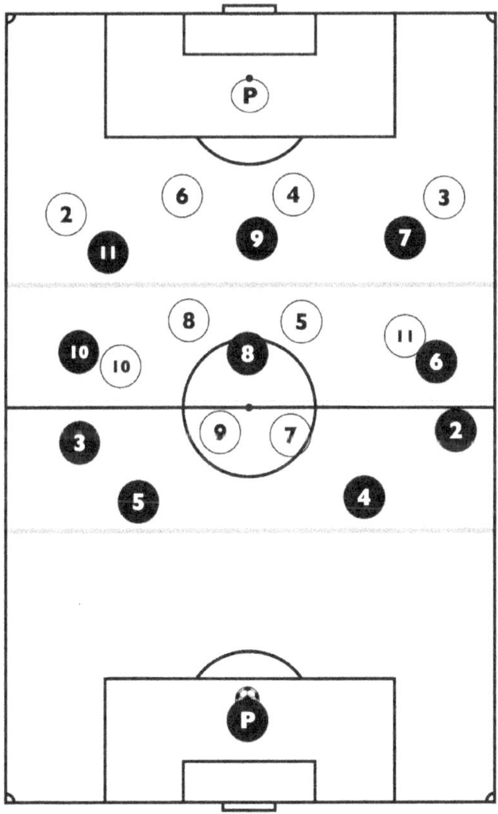

Drill N° 64	Main Objective	Defensive transition improvement
	Number of players	18

Explanation

A player on the white team (1) drives ball, and a player from the black team (2) comes out without a ball. Player 1 will attempt to pass the ball between the two cones, and Player 2 will try to prevent 1 from succeeding. When the action is over, a player will come out of another team (3) driving the ball and attempting the same action. And Player 2 will stay to press on player 3. And so on.

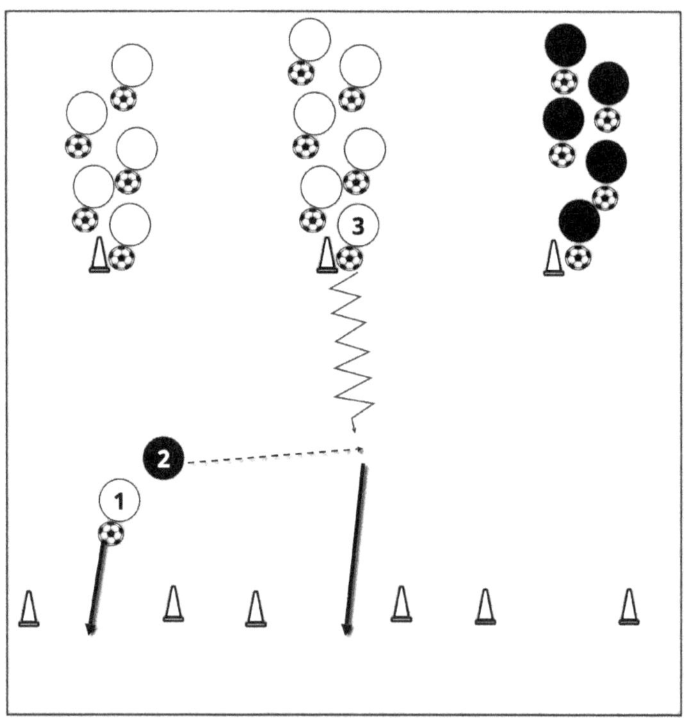

Drill N° 65	Main Objective	Ofensive transition improvement
	Number of players	4 (1+1x1+1)

Explanation

Players placed as shown in the picture. The player of the black team has the ball and when the white team steals, it must pass to the player in the other square. The center player can assist in the pressing, or stay in the aisle to intercept the pass.

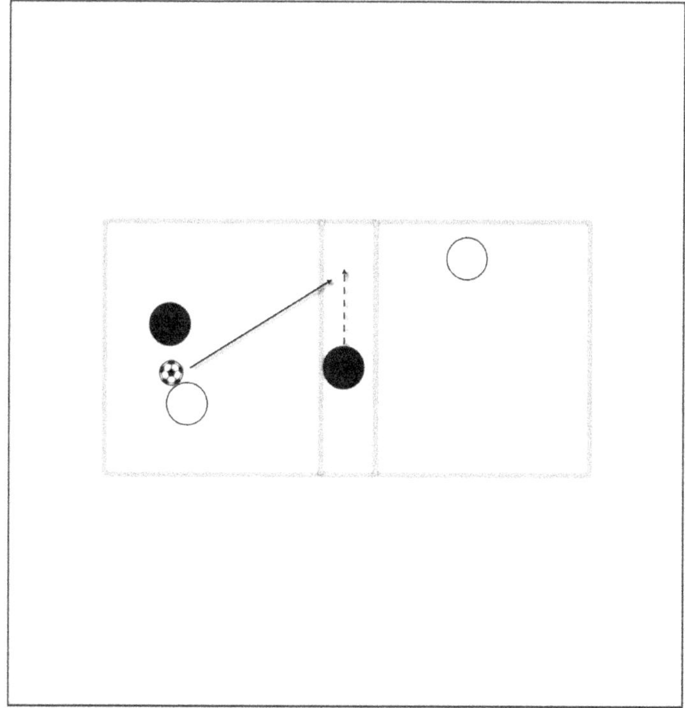

Drill N° 66	Main Objective	Ofensive transition improvement
	Number of players	5 (P+2x1+1)

Explanation

Players distributed as shown in the picture. 1 has the ball, and if he loses it, he'll press player 3. Player 2 will decide whether to also press Player 3, if he stays on the line to intercept the pass, or if he is going to mark to player 4, to prevent the white team.

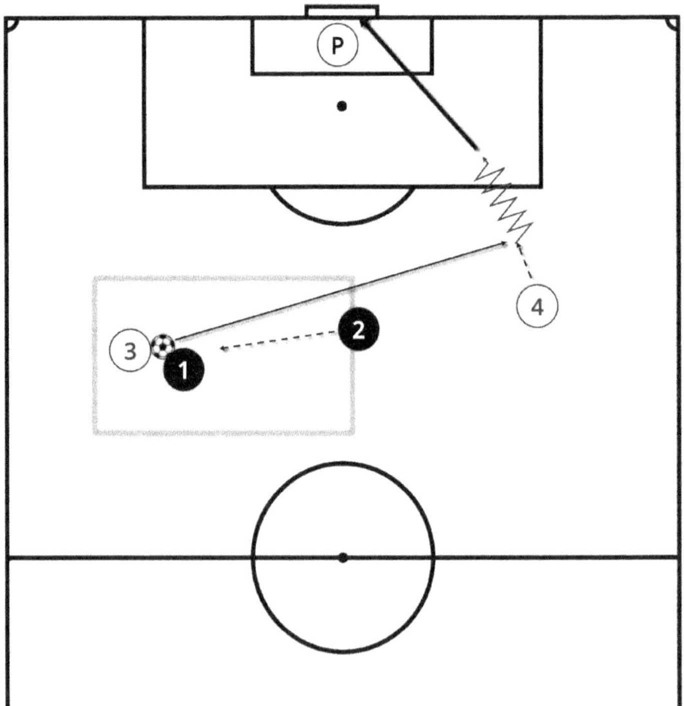

Drill N° 67	Main Objective	Defensive transition improvement
	Number of players	7

Explanation

Players distributed as shown in the picture. 1 has the ball. 2 presses 1, and when he steals the ball, he will pass it on to one of the teammates in the middle and the two will attack the goal. 1 and 3 defend the attack.

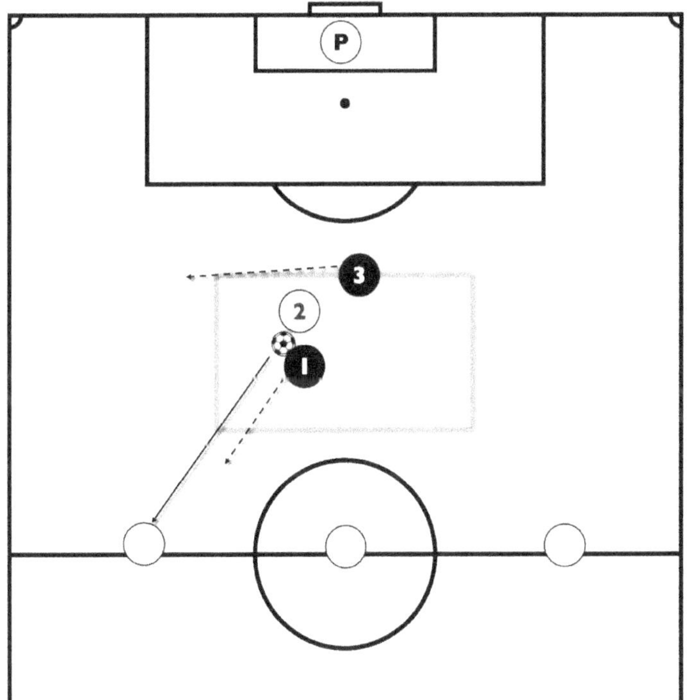

Drill N° 68	Main Objective	Defensive transition improvement
	Number of players	10

Explanation

Three players attack (black team) and one defends (white player). When the action ends, more players from the white team will enter the field and, aided by the white player who was already on the field, will attack the other goal. Players on the black team will be left close to press the start of the attack. Rotate the number of white players attacking on each move (2,3,4…).

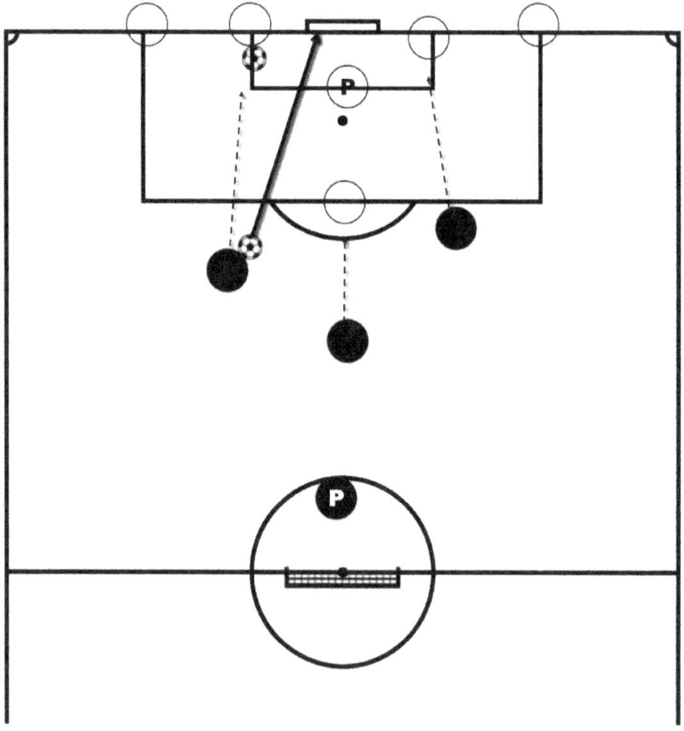

Drill N° 69	Main Objective	Defensive transition improvement
	Number of players	8

Explanation

Players placed as shown in the picture. The black team is passing the ball between them. When ball is passed to the player who is furthest from the goal, the white team will be able to intercept the pass and attack towards the goal. From one action to another, the white team will rotate the number of players attacking, and the point from which they come out. The black team, when losing the ball, will press so that the white team does not score.

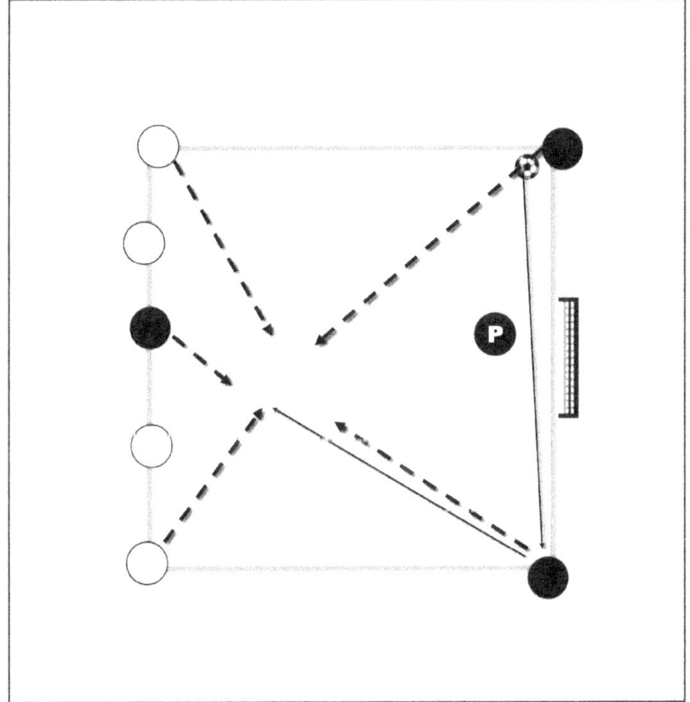

Drill N° 70	Main Objective	Defensive transition improvement
	Number of players	11

Explanation

Players placed as shown in the picture. The black team will pass the ball between them inside, and when a player from the white team intercepts the ball, four players from the white team will enter to attack. Rotate which players are the players who enter each action. The black team, when losing the ball, will press that the white team does not score.

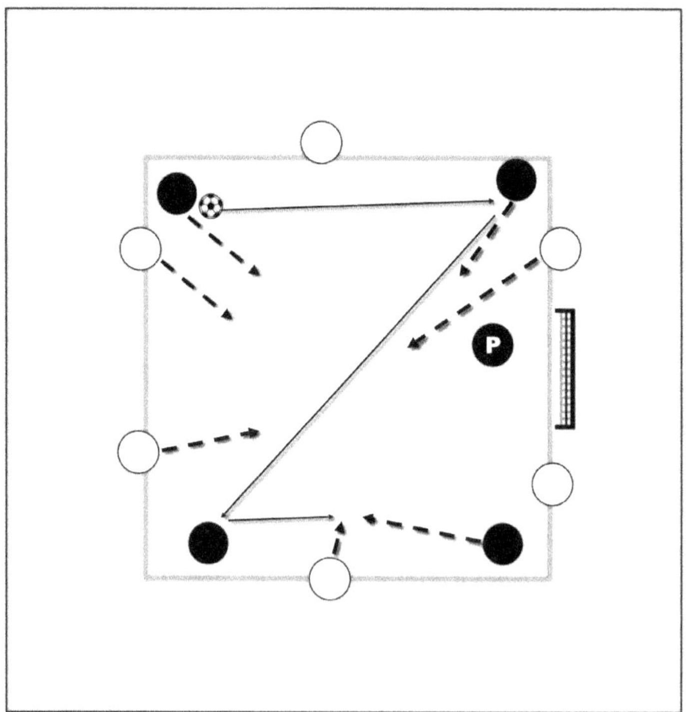

Drill N° 71	Main Objective	Defensive transition improvement
	Number of players	8

Explanation

Players placed as shown in the picture. The black team is passing the ball between them. When ball is passed to the player who is furthest from the goal, the white team will be able to intercept the pass and attack towards the goal. From one action to another, the white team will rotate the number of players attacking, and the point from which they come out. The black team, when losing the ball, will press so that the white team does not score.

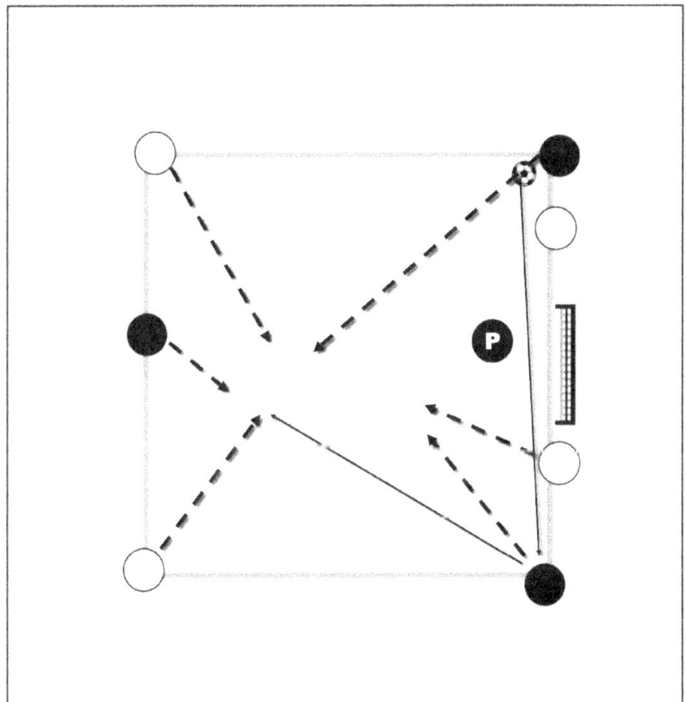

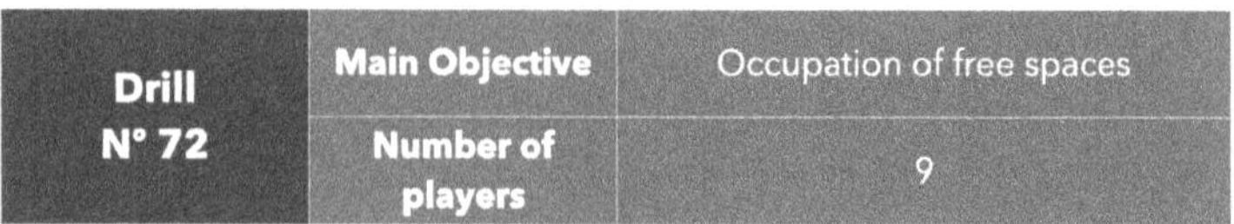

Drill N° 72	Main Objective	Occupation of free spaces
	Number of players	9

Explanation

Players distributed as shown in the picture. Player 1 will move on to his teammate 2, the one who is furthest from the goal, and then the players of the black team enter the square to press. White player 2 will pass the ball to one of his teammates who has been unchecked to receive the ball and initiate an attack. From one action to another, change the white players that come in to attack.

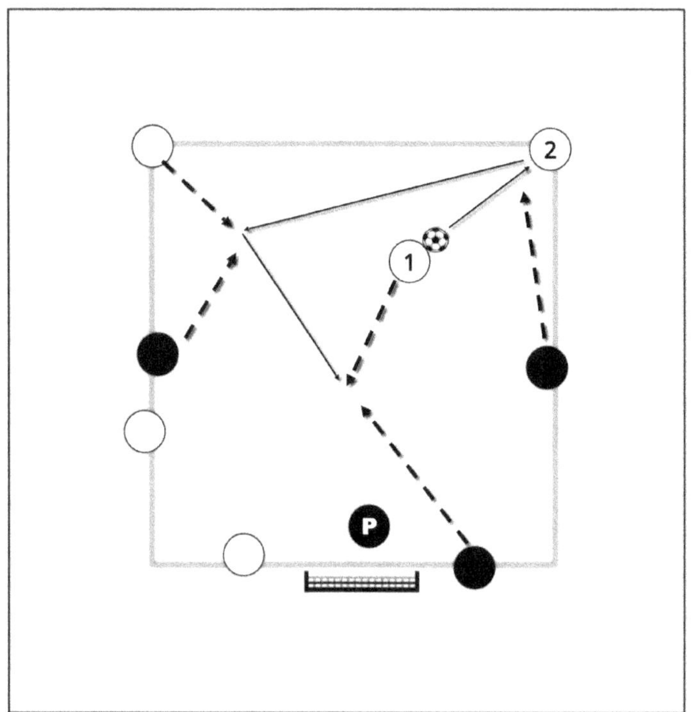

Drill N° 73	Main Objective	Attract to pass
	Number of players	18 (8x8+2C)

Explanation

The playing field, as shown in the picture. There is one player from each team in each of the 8 small fields. The white team has ball possession. The neutral players (C) will have freedom of movement, and will always participate with the team who has ball possession. The black team is the defending team. Players on the black team will be able to leave their square to help a teammate who is trying to recover the ball, and who is in numerical inferiority. The white team, once it attracts a rival, will have freed a partner and will continue to pass the ball.When the black team retrieves the ball, there will be a change of roles between the two teams.

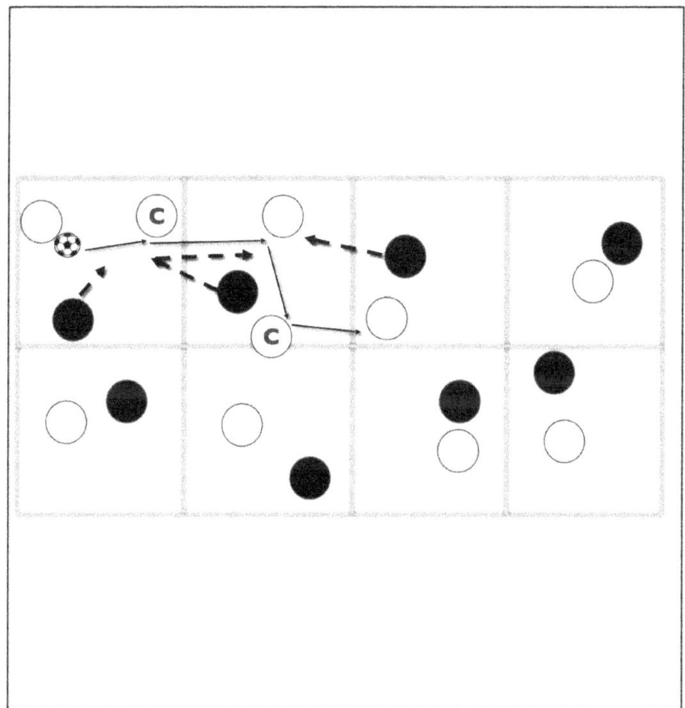

Drill N° 74	Main Objective	Zonal defense
	Number of players	14

Explanation

The playing field, and the players, as shown in the picture. The attacking team passes and passes the ball, until it finds an option to pass to the most advanced player. If he receives, defenders will be able to press him to avoid or hinder the shooting. The attacking teams will tuck, between the opponent's defensive line, one or two players to distract the defenders.

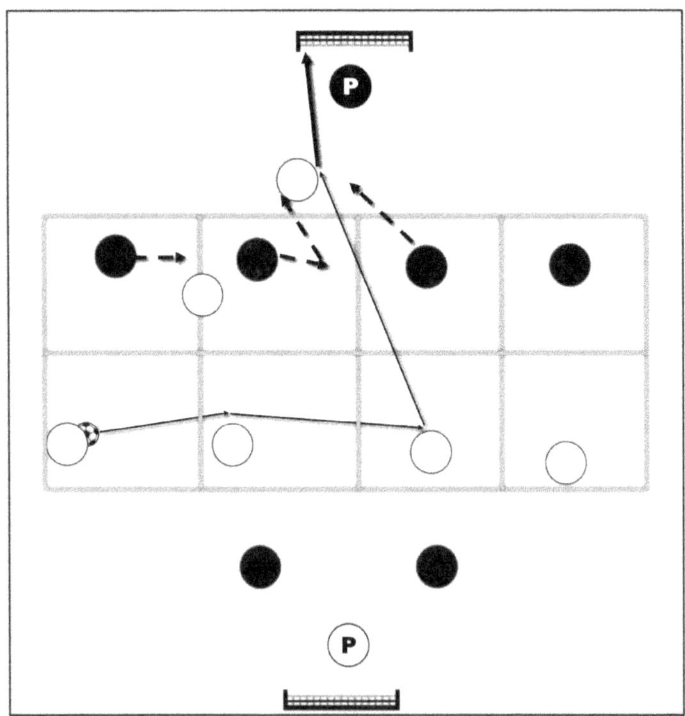

Drill N° 75	Main Objective	Ball possesion improvement
	Number of players	12 (P+5x5+P)

Explanation

One team attacks and another defends. The defending team uses a different structure in each attack, but always on two lines (3-2, 2-3, 4-1 or 1-4). And when the attacking team loses the ball, it will defend its goal under a different structure than the one it faced.

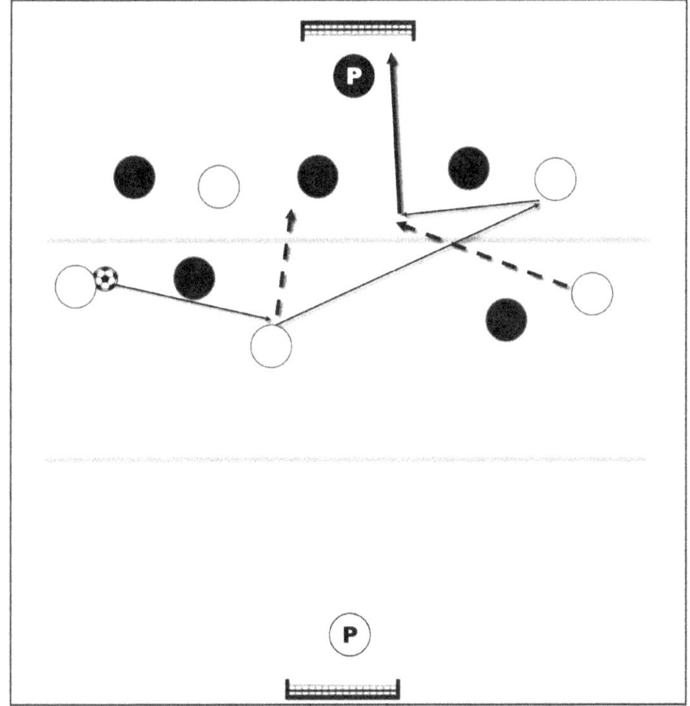

Drill N° 76	Main Objective	Ball possesion improvement
	Number of players	9 (4x4+C)

Explanation

Players placed as shown in the picture. The black team has ball possession. Players on the white team will be able to press and have freedom of movement to steal the ball. Black team players will each remain in their square, and keep possession, aided by the neutral player (C), always looking for the free player. When they lose the ball, teams change roles.

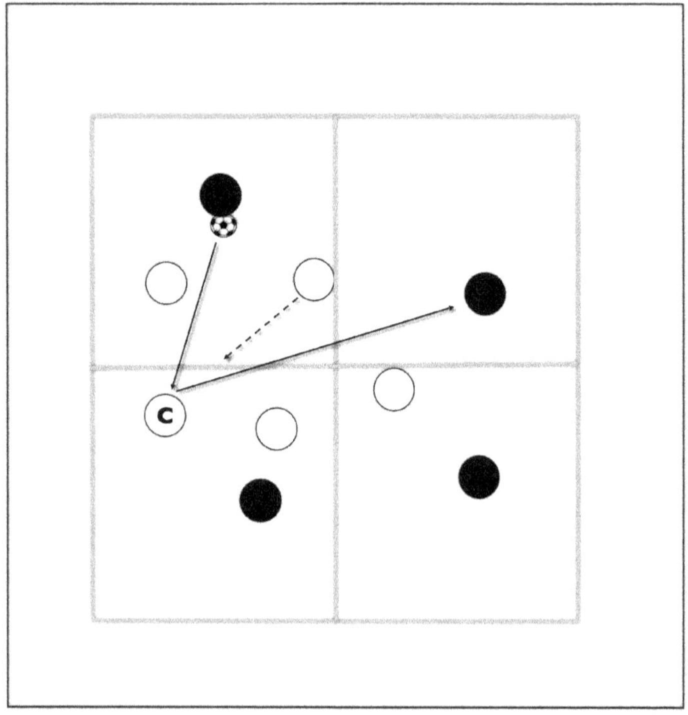

Drill N° 77	Main Objective	Ball possesion improvement
	Number of players	16 (4C+4x4+4)

Explanation

Players distributed as shown in the picture. One team keeping possession the ball, and two other teams press and attempt to steal it. When the ball is in a square, only one player from each defending team can press. When the ball comes out of that square, the players of the defending teams will return to their starting points. Roles are changed when a team retrieves the ball.

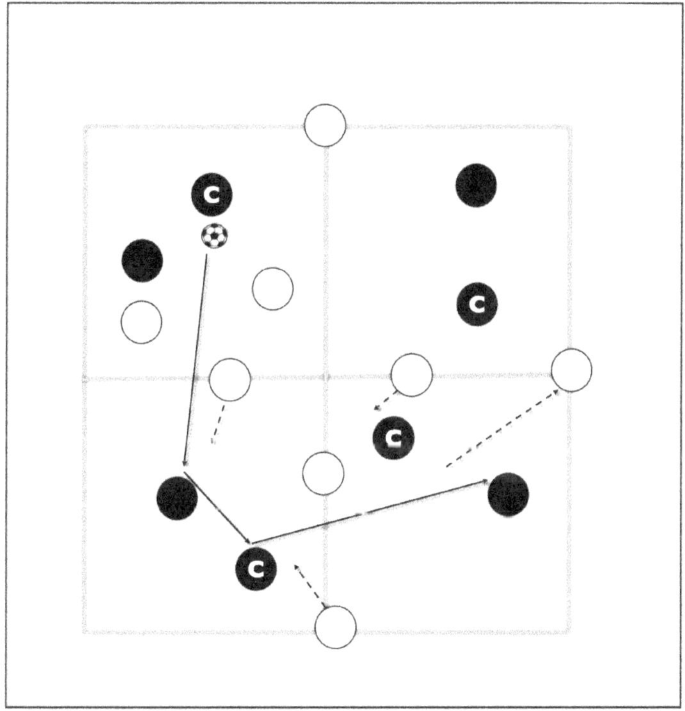

Drill N° 78	Main Objective	Attract to pass
	Number of players	10 (P+4x4+P)

Explanation

Players distended as shown in the picture. The players of the team in possession can change their place to attract rivals. The team that does not have the ball (white) will coordinate to enter the square to be pressed (each time a different number of players). The other team (black) will attract the opponent, and when the players of the white team come to press, the players of the black team will play with their most advanced teammates, in order to attack the goal. If the black team steals the ball, try to score. Then the roles change.

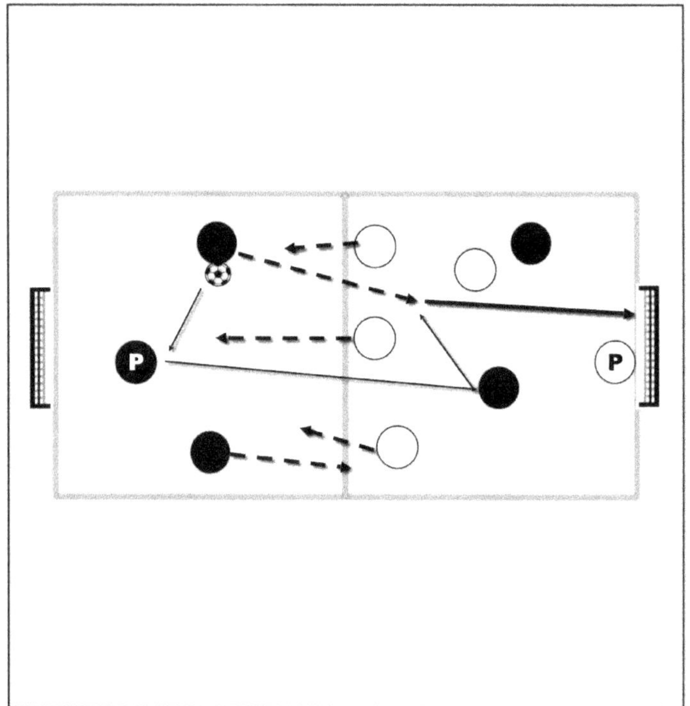

Drill N° 79	Main Objective	Get out of pressing
	Number of players	9 (4x4+C)

Explanation

A team has the ball, and causes the opponent to enter to press in the square. The team outside coordinates to enter to press, leaving one or more players among the squares to intercept, and when they do the team that has the ball will play with the neutral player of the other square. If a single player enters to press, they can pass the ball to the other square. When the neutral player receive the ball, he will leave the ball there, and go to the other square. Again, the other team will have to enter to press on the other square (leaving players, to intercept) and the white team will pass the ball. If they steal or intercept the ball, they will change the roles.

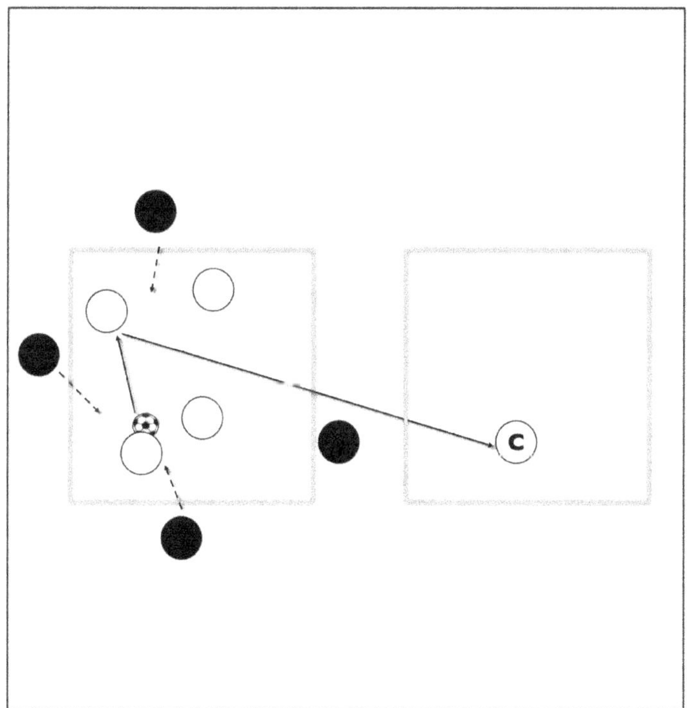

Drill N° 80	Main Objective	Defensive transition improvement
	Number of players	10 (5x5)

Explanation

Field as shown the picture. The team that does not have the ball (black) will attempt to intercept a pass from the white team and, when it does, some players will go to the other field to receive the ball, and others will stay as support for the player they intercepted. The idea is to try to play the ball with the most advanced players and keep possession in the rectangle. The white team, when losing the ball, will have to be ordered defensively watching of the remaining players on each field, and try to recover the ball in the shortest possible time. The distribution of the team that try recover, will not always be the same.

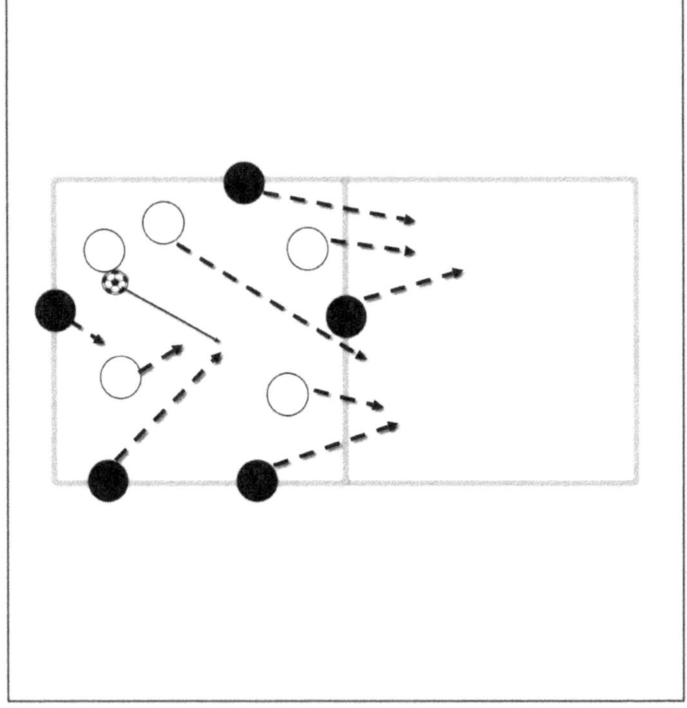

Drill N° 81	Main Objective	Ofensive transition improvement
	Number of players	7

Explanation

Players distributed as shown in the picture. Players pass one at a time by driving ball across the big square, passing through the small square. The players will have to go one at a time, and from side to side, passing through the square of the center. The player without the ball will attempt to steal the ball from those who pass through "his" squared. When he steals ball, he'll shoot at goal with the pressure of one of the vertex players. The one who lost go to the square, and will wait to steal the players who pass by.

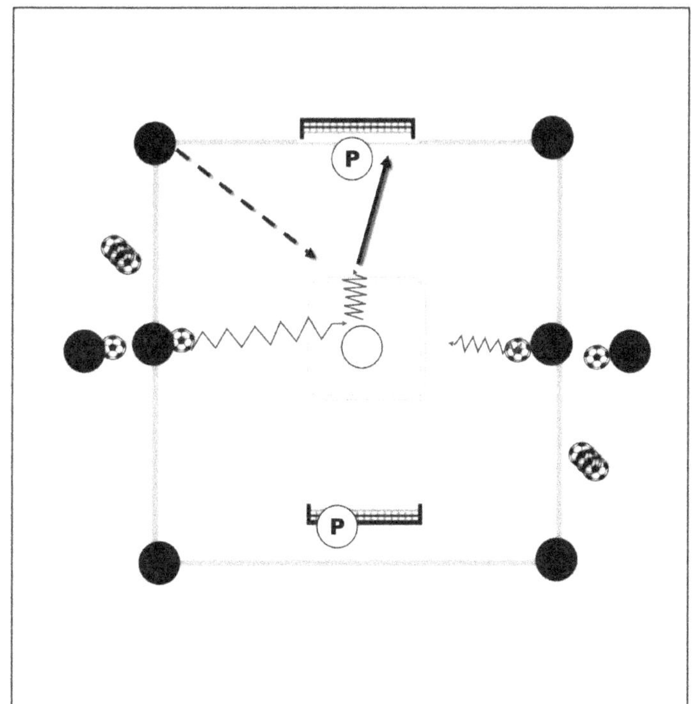

Drill N° 82	Main Objective	Attract to pass
	Number of players	10

Explanation

Players distributed as shown in the picture. The two players in the center have the ball to attract two opposing players who will press them (they will change the place from which they will press each time). When they go to pressure, they can play with one of the corner mates to attack one of the goals.

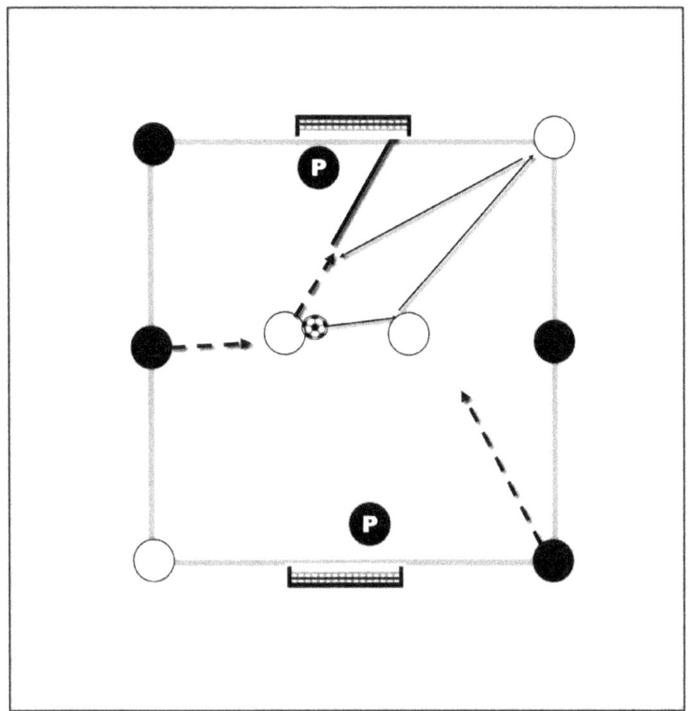

Drill N° 83	Main Objective	Ofensive transition improvement
	Number of players	11 (5x5+P)

Explanation

In a rectangle divided into two squares, players are placed as shown in the picture. The black team will attempt to intercept a pass from the white team, and when it does, some players will go to the other field to receive and others will stay to support the player who intercepted the pass. The white team when they lose will have to order defensively attending to the players that remain in each field not to receive goal. Vary the distributions of players on the field to give variability to situations.

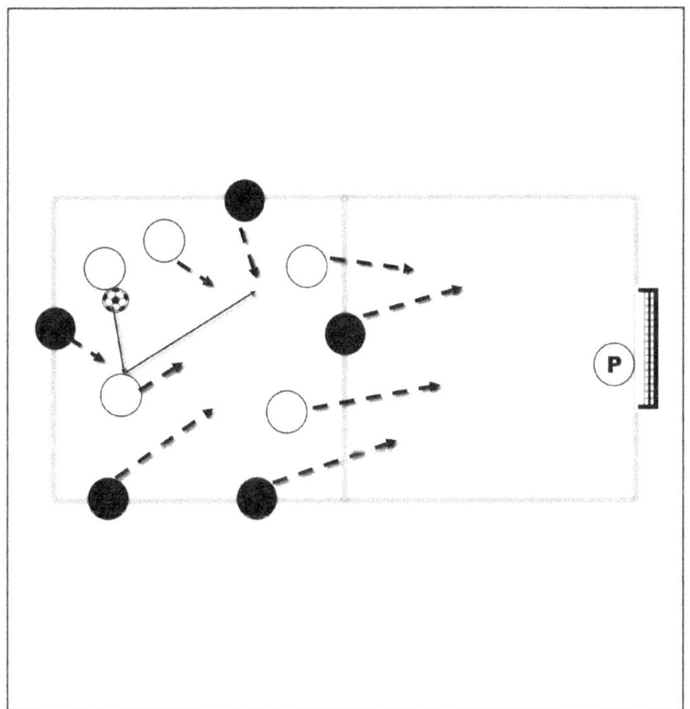

Drill N° 84	Main Objective	Attract to pass
	Number of players	9

Explanation

Players distributed as shown in the picture. The player from the center has the ball and tries to attract two opposing players who will press him (they will alternate the place from which they will). When they go to press, he can play with one of the corner teammates to attack one of the goals.

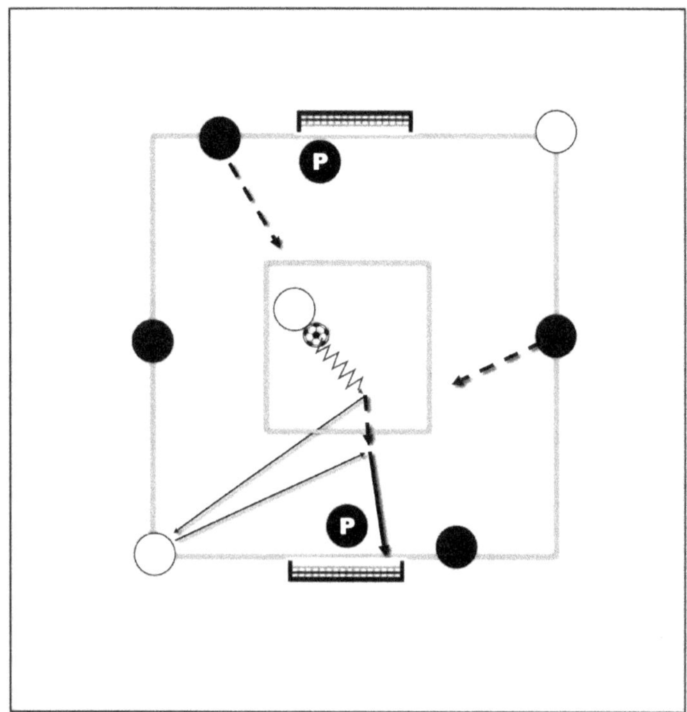

Drill N° 85	Main Objective	Attract to pass
	Number of players	9

Explanation

Players distributed as shown in the picture. The player from the center has the ball and tries to attract two opposing players who will press him (they will alternate the place from which they will). When they go to press, the player with the ball can play with cornermates to make a 3x2 attack.

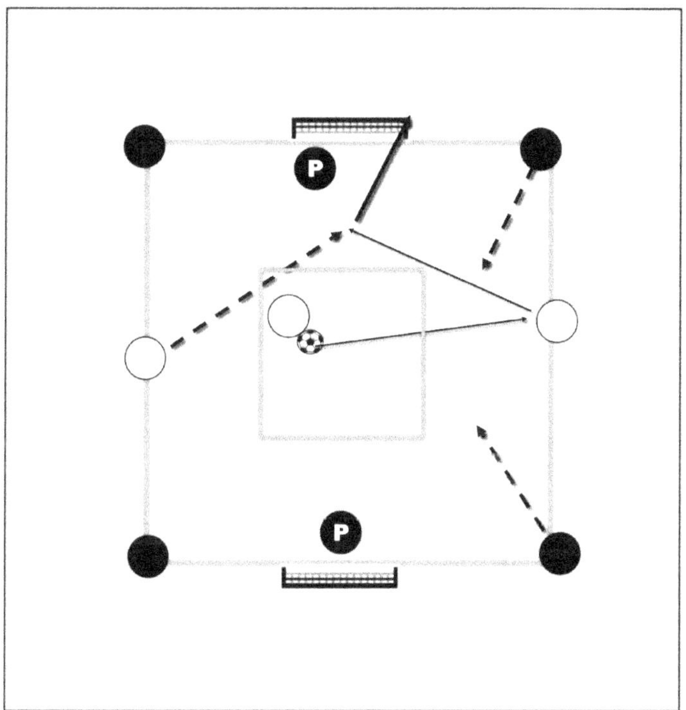

Drill N° 86	Main Objective	Attract to pass
	Number of players	15

Explanation

Players are distributed as shown in the picture. Four players play (black team). When players on the white team come to press, players on the black team move on to one of the two players outside, they go out to attack and the entire black team will attack the goal defended by the goalkeeper and white players who stayed out.

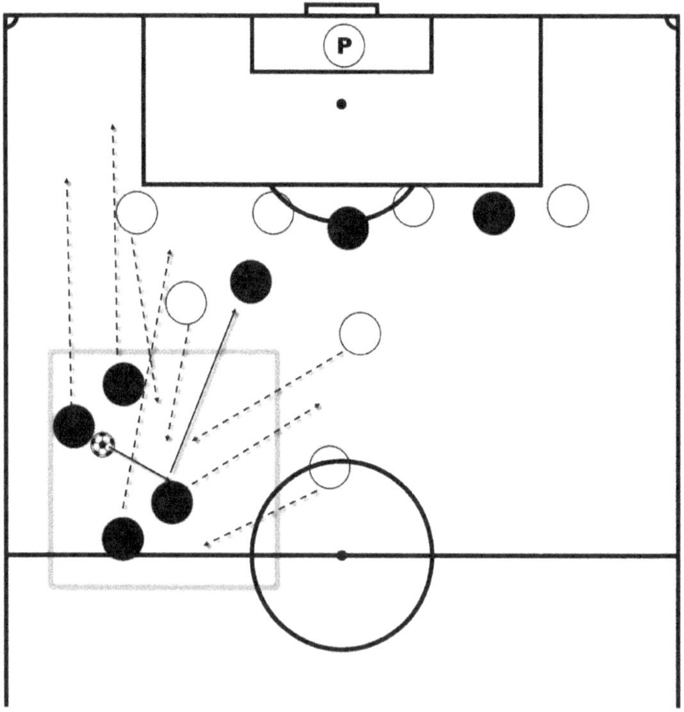

Drill N° 87	Main Objective	Ofensive transition improvement
	Number of players	10 (4+Px4+P)

Explanation

4x4. Each time a team attacks, the player who shot to goal or loses the ball, will have to go to one of the cones on the opposing baseline. And the other team will make a counterattack before the rival team is ordered.

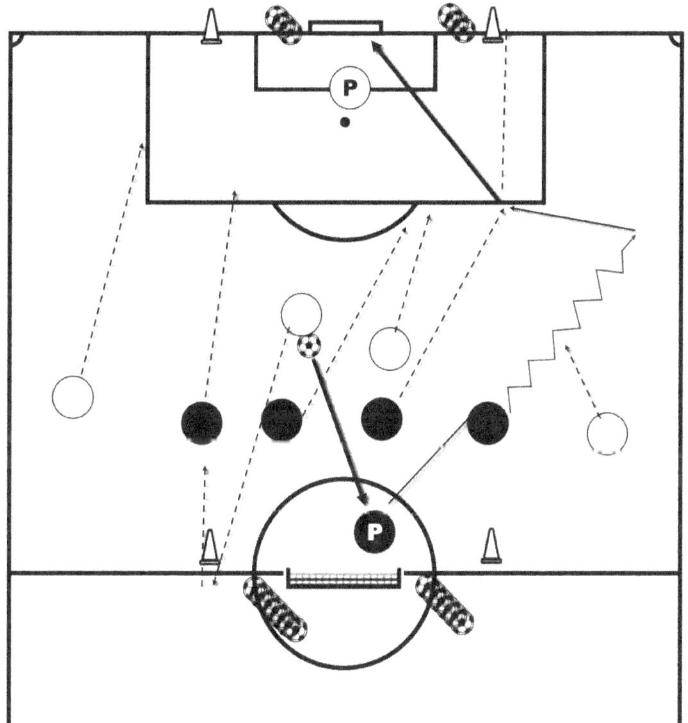

Drill N° 88	Main Objective	Ofensive transition improvement
	Number of players	10 (4+Px4+P)

Explanation

4x4. Each time a team attacks, the player who shot to goal or loses the ball, and other teammate, will have to go to one of the cones on the opposing baseline. And the other team will make a counterattack before the rival team is ordered.

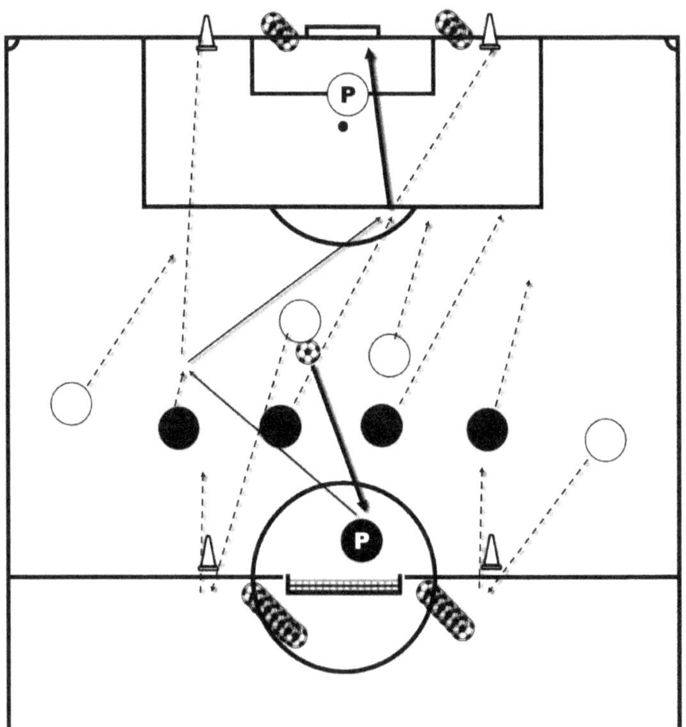

Drill N° 89	Main Objective	Defensive and ofensive transitions improvement
	Number of players	12

Explanation

5x4 as shown in the picture. When a team steals the ball, it plays with the player who did not defend (who will be looking for the best disposition). And the player who loses or throws to goal, does not participate in defence and stay waiting for his team to retrieve the ball, or that opponent finish and play with him to take advantage of the spaces behind him. The defensive fall-back, will be done with one player in each aisle.

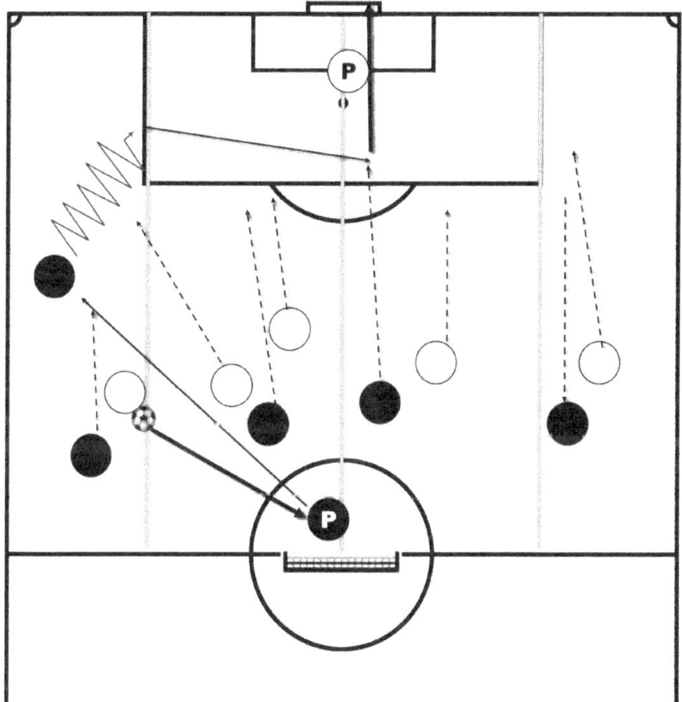

Drill N° 90	Main Objective	Ofensive transition improvement
	Number of players	22

Explanation

The field marked as shown in the picture. When a team lose the ball or finish a play, all players will retreat behind the line minus a number of players who will stay pressing. This players will be randomly alternated (not always the same, and not always the same number)

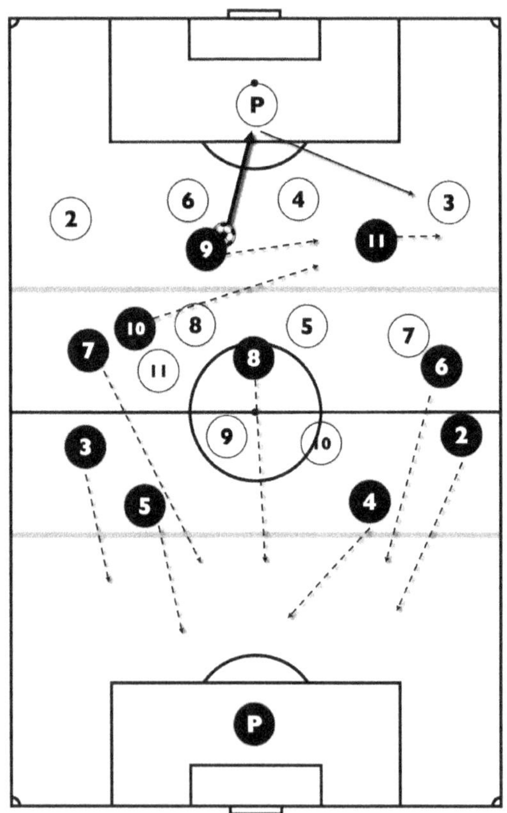

Drill N° 91	Main Objective	Defensive transition and ball possession improvement
	Number of players	22

Explanation

The field marked as shown in the picture. When a team lose the ball or finish a play, players will form a defensive line over the line of their field of 3, 4 or 5 players (not always the same, and not always the same number). The team that stole the ball, make a counterattack or an organized attack.

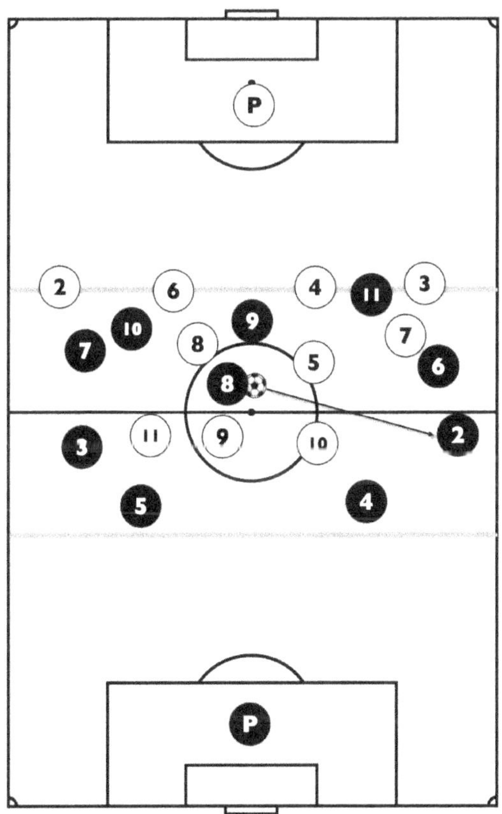

Drill N° 92	Main Objective	Ofensive transition improvement
	Number of players	22 (10+Px10+P)

Explanation

Match 11x11. The two teams will press the opposing team with man-marking across the field, each time a ball loss occurs. The marks may not be the same every time the ball is lost, alternating the pairing.

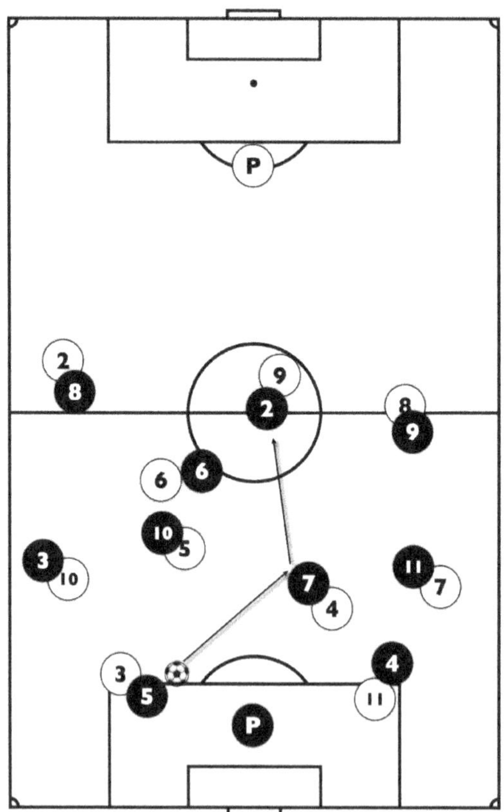

Drill N° 93	Main Objective	Transitions and ball possession improvemente
	Number of players	22

Explanation

11x11. The field marked as in the image. The defending teams will be distributed over the 3 lines closest to their goal, alternating the structure on each of them each time they lose the ball. Defending players must remain on the lines, and will only be able to intercept passes..

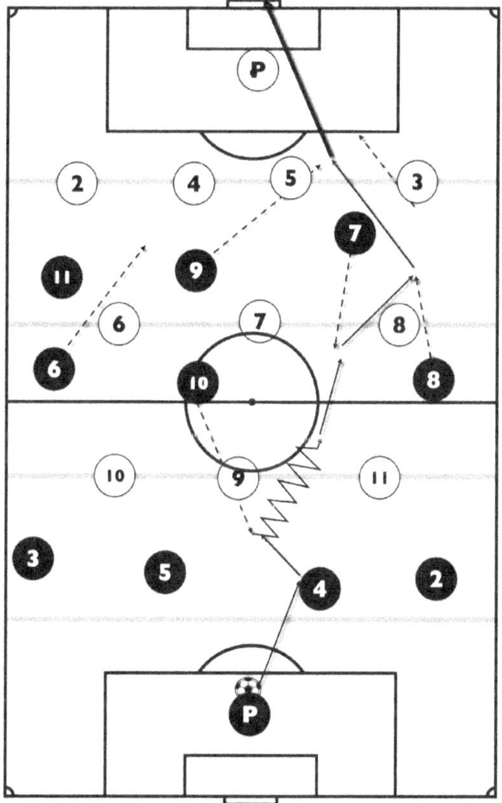

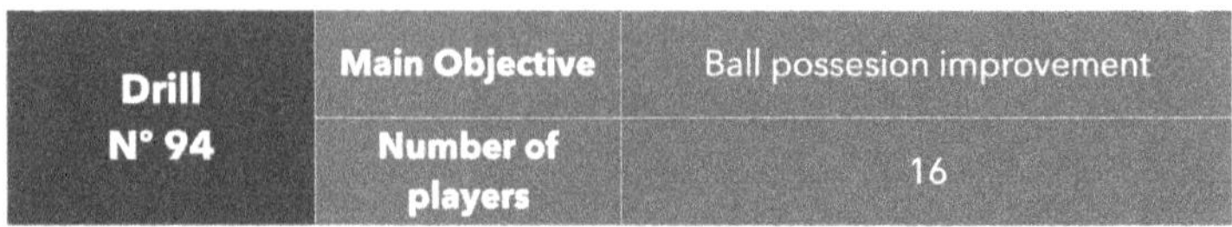

Drill N° 94	Main Objective	Ball possesion improvement
	Number of players	16

Explanation

Field as shown in the picture. In a rectangle divided into three equal fields, the teams are distributed: 3 in the central area and 1 over the line. Players on the lines will only be able to intercept passes in defense, in attack they will expect their teammates to attract opponents to receive in depth and attack the rival goal. When they do, they will be able to randomly enter one or two players by the coach to defend, changing the number and disposition of the players who come to defend in each attack.

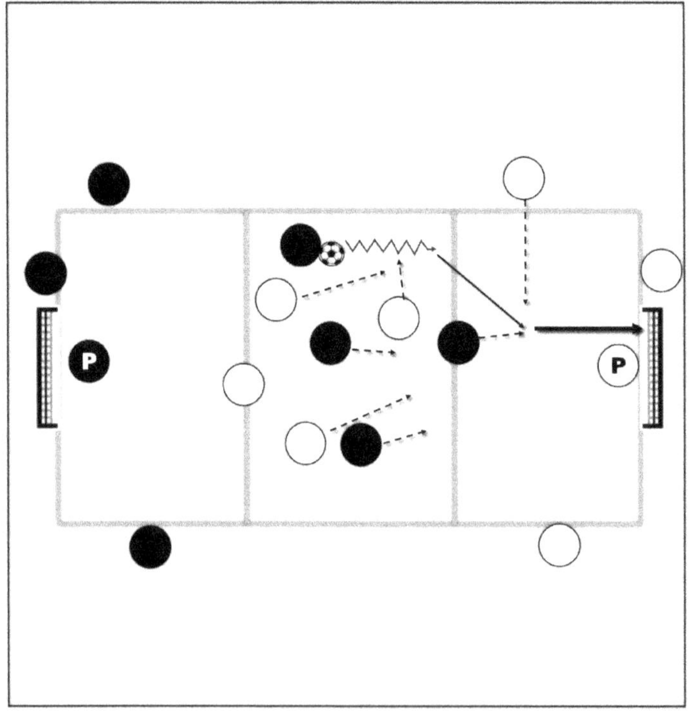

Drill N° 95	Main Objective	Ball possesion improvement
	Number of players	12

Explanation

Field as shown in the picture. In the central area there will be 2 players from each team. Over the defensive line, there are 3 players from the attacking team, and 1 from the defending team. Players on the line of the attacking team will be added to forward positions randomly, but never two players at once. The defending player will be watching the players who join the attack. If a team recovers the ball, the two players who were off the line will be incorporated, and two of the team that lost the ball will be taken out.

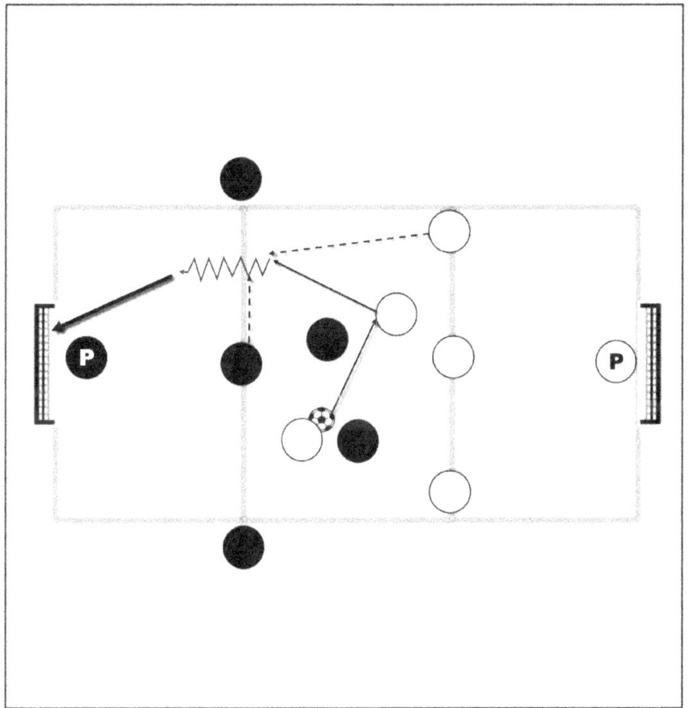

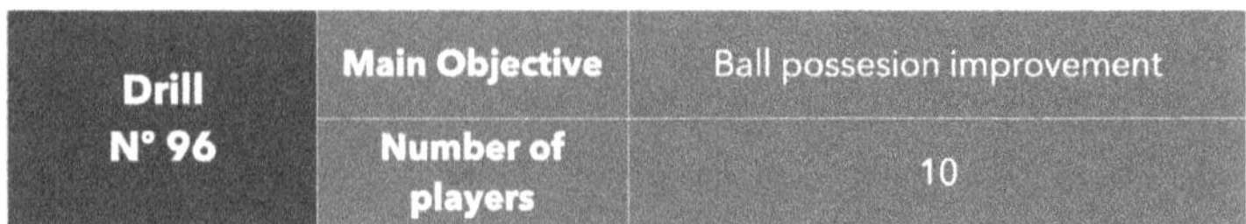

Drill N° 96	Main Objective	Ball possesion improvement
	Number of players	10

Explanation

Field as shown in the picture. Players in a one-on-one situation in the center will try to pass the ball to the back mate. And players outside will be able to enter the aisles to intercept the passes, but they won't be able to stay in them.

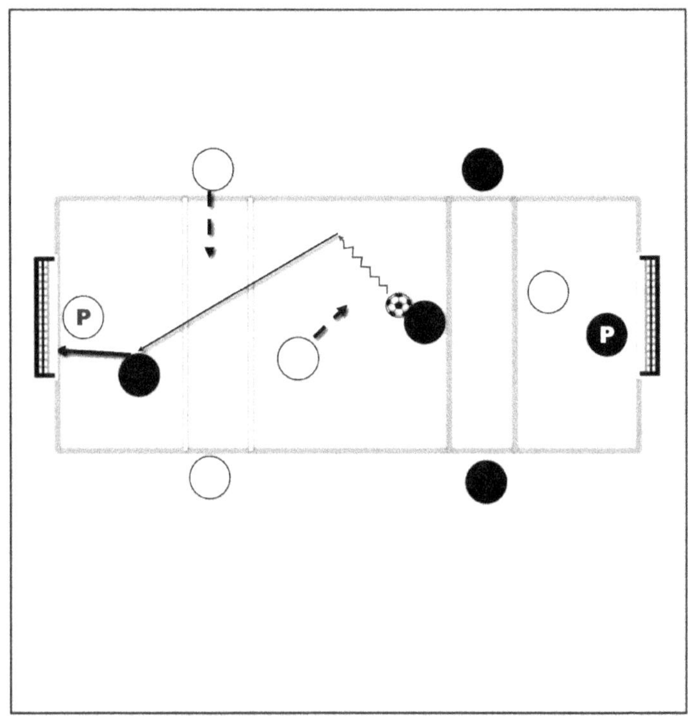

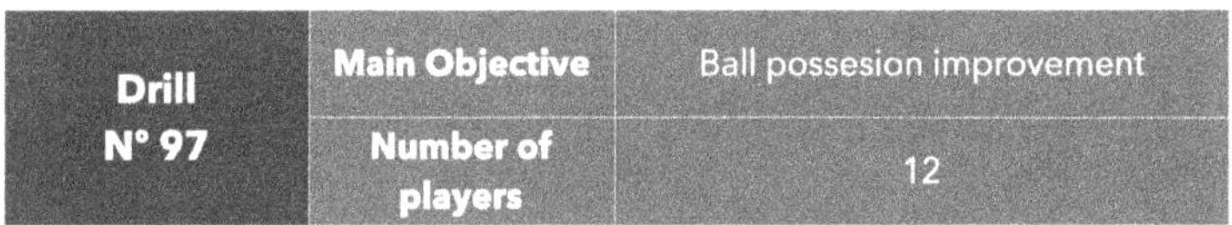

Drill N° 97	Main Objective	Ball possesion improvement
	Number of players	12

Explanation

Players distibuted as shown in the picture. Players in 1v1 situations in the center will try to pass the aisle partner. Players who are outside will be able to enter the central area randomly (but only one), to press the player who wants to shot. If they recover the ball, they pass ball to the center to play with the aislemate.

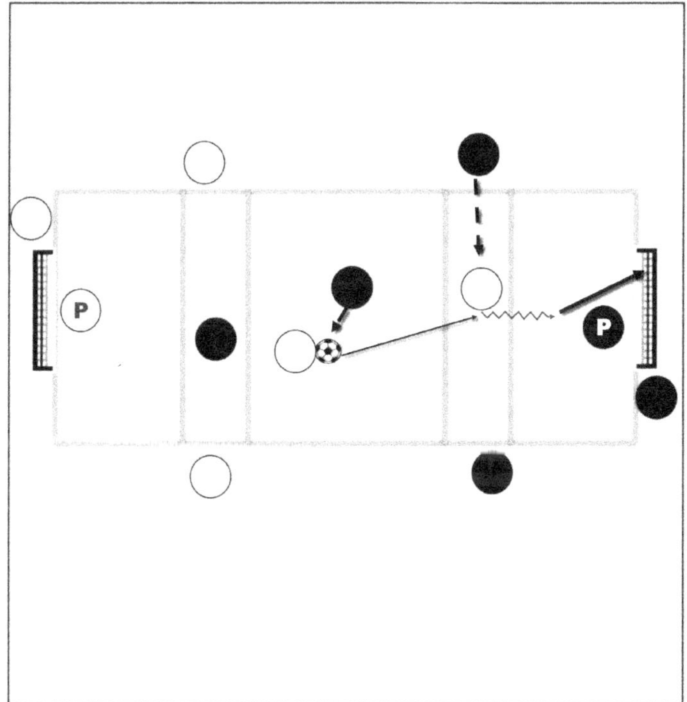

Drill N° 98	Main Objective	Defensive vigilance improvement
	Number of players	10

Explanation

Players distibuted as shown in the picture, three in the center zone and one over the line. Players on the lines will only be able to intercept passes in defense, and in attack they will provide support. Players who are on the outside lines will offer support constantly and randomly when their team has the ball, will be watched and pressed by the rival players of the lines.

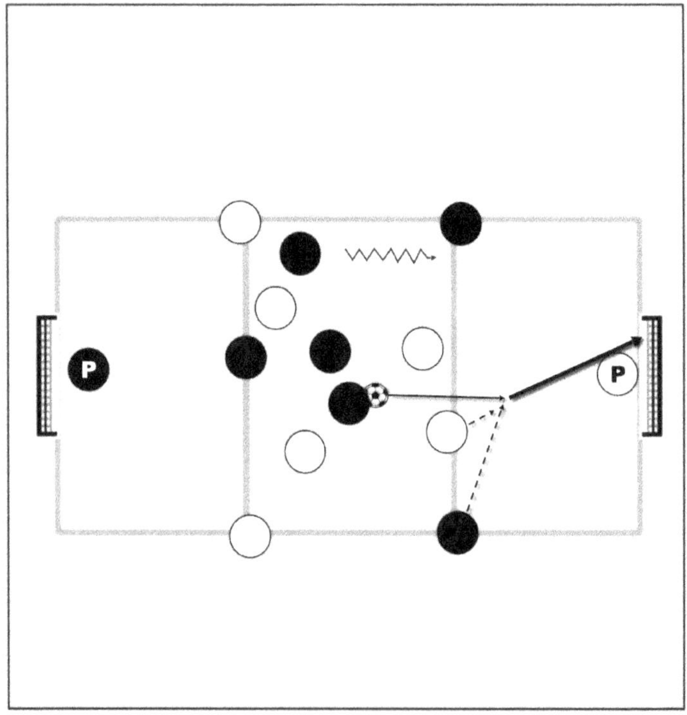

Drill N° 99	Main Objective	Improve playing with and without the ball
	Number of players	16

Explanation

A team will attack the goal. The goal will be defended each time by a different defensive line (two, three, four or five players). Those who pass the ball will be pressed by rival players who are not on the defensive line. Only players who passed the ball in the rondo will be able to attack, and who also managed to move to the other area before a player passes from one area to another driving the ball.

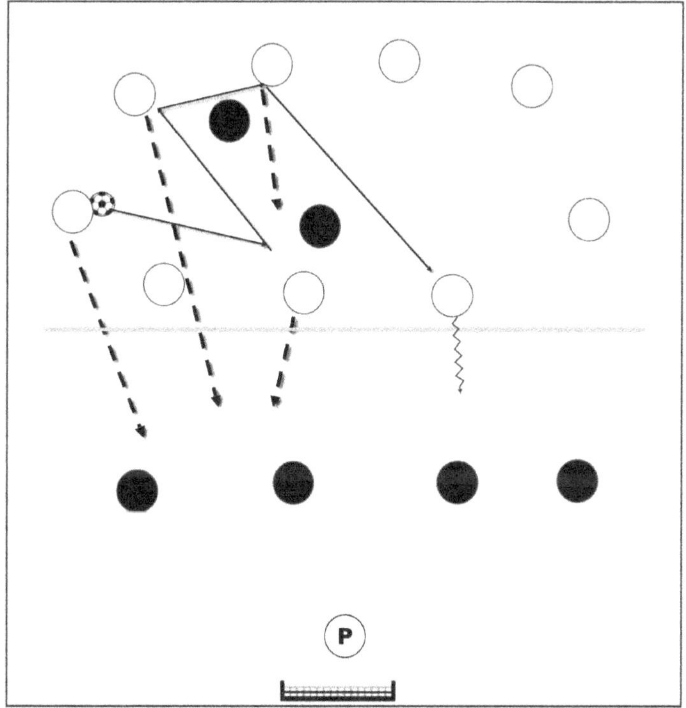

Drill N° 100	Main Objective	Zonal defense improvement
	Number of players	18

Explanation

Players as shown in the picture. Players on the white team passing the ball (pressed by three players from the black team) will exit the rectangle when each one passes and will be placed in a position to attack. The four players on the black team that form the line will prepare to defend the goal when one of the white players who came out, receives the ball. When the white team feels pressured (and before losing the ball) it will play with one of the outside players to attack (only those who passed and left).

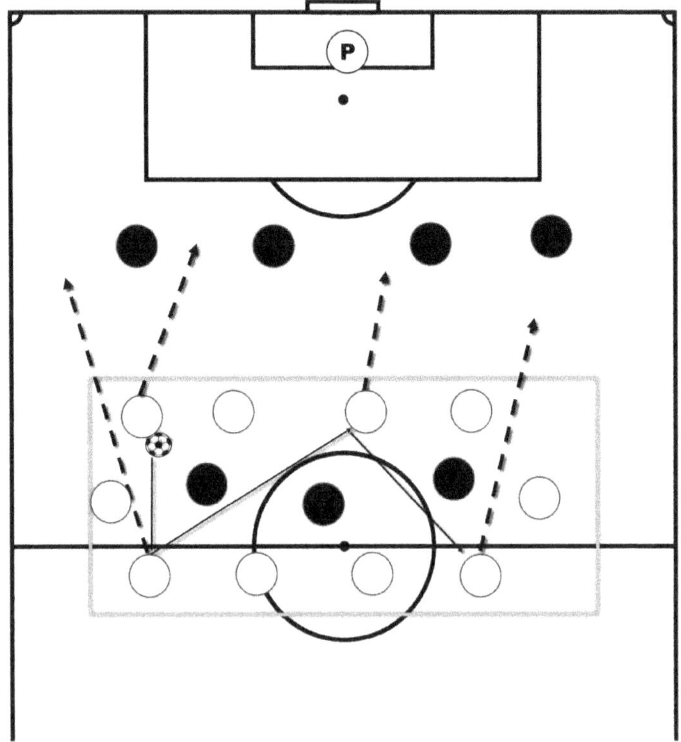

BIBLIOGRAFÍA

- Alarcón, F.; Cárdenas, D.; Clemente, V.; Collado, J. A. (Coord.); Guillén, J. C.; Jiménez, M.; Lázaro J.; Mercadé, O.; Ardoy, D. N.; Rivilla, I. y Sánchez, M. (2018): *Neurociencia, deporte y educación.* Editorial Wanceulen.

- Ballarini, F. (2016): *REC: Porqué recordamos lo que recordamos y olvidamos lo que olvidamos.* Editorial Debate.

- Bangsbo, J. y Peitersen, B. (2002): *Fútbol: Jugar en defensa.* Editorial Paidotribo. Barcelona.

- Bargh, J. (2018): ¿Porqué hacemos lo que hacemos?: el poder del inconsciente. Editorial Ediciones B.

- Caballero, M. (2017): *Neuroeducación de profesores y para profesores: De profesor a maestro de cabecera.* Editorial Ediciones Pirámide.

- Caneda, R. (1999): *La zona en Fútbol.* Editorial Wanceulen. Sevilla.

- Cano Moreno, Oscar (2010): *Fútbol: Entrenamiento global basado en la interpretación del juego.* Editorial Wanceulen.

- Castellano, Julen y Casamichana, David (2016): *El arte de planificar en fútbol,* Editorial Futbol de libro.

- Castellano, Julen; Casamichana, David y San Román, Jaime (2015): *Los juegos reducidos en el entrenamiento del fútbol.* Editorial Futbol de libro.

- Castelo, J. (1999): *Futbol. Estructura y dinámica del juego.* Editorial INDE. Barcelona.

- Couto, A. (2015): *Las grandes escuelas del Fútbol Moderno.* Editorial Fútbol de libro.

- Espar, Xesco (2010): *Jugar con el corazón: La excelencia no es suficiente.* Plataforma Editorial.

- Fradua, Luis (1997): *La visión periférica del futbolista.* Editorial Paidotribo.

- García Ocaña, Francisco (2008): *Fútbol y Fútbol sala: 250 actividades sociomotrices.* Editorial Paidotribo. Barcelona.

- Garganta, J. y Pinto, J. en Graça, A. y Oliveira, J. (1997): *La enseñanza de los juegos Deportivos.* Editorial Paidotribo.

- González, Alberto (2013): *Fútbol. Dinámica del juego desde la perspectiva de las transiciones.* Editorial Learning 11.

- Jackson, Phil (2014): *Once anillos.* Editorial Roca.

- López López, Javier (2008): *Fútbol: Alevines: 120 fichas de sesiones de entrenamiento.* Editorial Wanceulen. Sevilla.

- López López, Javier (2008): *Fútbol: Cadetes: 160 fichas de sesiones de entrenamiento.* Editorial Wanceulen. Sevilla.

- López López, Javier (2009): *400 tareas integradas para el entrenamiento de la táctica ofensiva.* Editorial Wanceulen.

- López López, Javier (2009): *500 juegos para el entrenamiento físico con balón.* Editorial Wanceulen.

- López López, Javier (2009): *Fundamentos tácticos defensivos.* Editorial Wanceulen.

- López López, Javier (2009): Fútbol: *1380 Juegos globales para el aprendizaje y perfeccionamiento de la técnica ofensiva y defensiva.* Editorial Wanceulen. Sevilla.

- López López, Javier (2009): *Fútbol: Prebenjamines: 80 fichas de sesiones de entrenamiento.* Editorial Wanceulen. Sevilla.

- López López, Javier (2013): *Fútbol: Benjamines: 80 fichas de sesiones de entrenamiento.* Editorial Wanceulen. Sevilla.

- López López, Javier (2013): *Fútbol: Infantiles: 120 fichas de sesiones de entrenamiento.* Editorial Wanceulen. Sevilla.

- López López, Javier (2013): *Fútbol: Juveniles: 160 fichas de sesiones de entrenamiento.* Editorial Wanceulen. Sevilla.

- López López, Javier (2013): *Fútbol: Senior (2013): 175 fichas de sesiones de entrenamiento.* Editorial Wanceulen. Sevilla.

- López López, Javier; Wanceulen Moreno, Antonio; Wanceulen Moreno, José F. y Bernal Ruiz, Javier (2009): *225 juegos para el entrenamiento integrado del pase en el fútbol.* Editorial Wanceulen.

- Marí, Pep (2011): Aprender de los campeones. Plataforma Editorial.

- Marí, Pep (2019): *Equipos campeones: Como convertir un buen equipo en uno mucho mejor*. Editorial Plataforma Impresa.

- Mayer, R. (1996): *Fichas de fútbol. 120 juegos de ataque y defensa*. Hispano Europea. Barcelona.

- Mora, F. (2014): *¿Cómo funciona el cerebro?* Alianza editorial.

- Mora, F. (2017): *Neuroeducación: sólo se puede aprender de aquello que se ama*. Alianza editorial.

- Pérez, Marcial (2019): *Mente Deportiva: Entrenar el cerebro para extender los límites del rendimiento*. Autoría Editorial.

- Recuelta Candón, Amalia (2016): *El cerebro decide*. Editorial Fútbol Táctico.

- Seirul´lo, F. (1999): *Criterios modernos del entrenamiento en el fútbol*. Revista Training Fútbol. Valladolid.